DO OR DIE

Survival for Nonprofits

Lee, James C/Do or die : survival for no
HD2741 .L43 C.1 STACKS 1974

HD 2741
L43   Lee, James C.
      Do or die

...EGE FOR HUMAN SERVICES
LIBRARY
345 HUDSON STREET
NEW YORK, N.Y. 10014

Copyright © 1974
TAFT PRODUCTS, INC.

All rights reserved. This book, or parts thereof, must not be used or reproduced in any manner without written permission. For information, address the publisher, Taft Products, Inc., 1000 Vermont Avenue, N.W., Washington, D.C. 20005

Library of Congress Card Number
74-84556
ISBN 0-914756-05-2

Printed in the United States of America

*This book is for Wendy
who never stopped believing it
was only a matter of time.*

TABLE OF CONTENTS

CHAPTER 1
Why this book . . . or, how nonprofit organizations fail 1

CHAPTER 2
Effective organization . . . or, how can you send a great cause up in a crate like that? 9

CHAPTER 3
Effective organization ii . . . or, beginning to put all the pieces together .. 21

CHAPTER 4
Nonprofit programs . . . or, why doesn't somebody <u>do</u> something? 39

CHAPTER 5
Paying for it . . . where the nonprofiit dollar comes from, and how to get it 51

CHAPTER 6
Ars gratia pecuniam . . . creativity in the nonprofit marketplace 67

CHAPTER 7
Effective organization, a reprise . . . or, back to the drawing board 79

CHAPTER 8
Toward a new beginning . . . the coming of age of nonprofit organizations 99

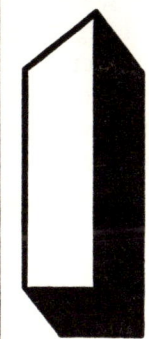

WHY THIS BOOK... OR, HOW NONPROFIT ORGANIZATIONS FAIL

The subject of this book is money. Specifically, it is about the medium of exchange that has come to be known as "the nonprofit dollar." For most of our society, the nonprofit dollar is a currency as exotic as any on the international money market. And there is little understanding of where it comes from, how it is earned, who's getting and spending it, and why.

Unfortunately, some of those who least understand the nonprofit dollar—and the marketplace in which it floats—are those charged with its stewardship. The reasons why this is so involve complex human emotions and attitudes which often tend to cloud more basic and more important issues which nonprofit organizations must face. But these attitudes and emotions must be unraveled and resolved before an already troubled nonprofit community sinks into confusion and futility. There are some hard realities of management and performance which nonprofits must face if they are to perform successfully the role they have accepted in our culture.

There is widespread—and justifiable—sentiment that nonprofit organizations perform a vital—and more often than not, thankless—task within society. There are those, especially in the nonprofit community, who would point out that there are millions of us who would be homeless, hungry, mentally unstable, and dying unnecessarily of crude diseases were it not for our nonprofit institutions. It is the callousness bred into us by an industrialized, semi-democratic technocracy, this argument goes, that makes it compulsory for our society to develop a collective, and organized conscience. Without these organizations, it is held, we might never resist the materialistic values of establishment America for a moment's concern for the outsiders, the have-nots. It is, in fact, this preoccupation with money that is the reason why our nonprofit organizations are necessary in the first place.

Almost, but not quite.

This book is not an attack on our nonprofit institutions, their motives, nor their work, any more than it is a defense of capitalism. It is directed toward those who are responsible for the management of the nonprofit dollar, and are most deeply committed to its wise and beneficial use. But if this book is to be of any value to executives in the nonprofit marketplace, they must first accept a simple axiom which many will find smacks of heresy: Concern for money is not evil. It can even be a good thing. And when it comes to managing money effectively, the philanthropic community has much to learn from "the materialistic values of establishment America."

Increasingly, the word "nonprofit" has come to mean "antiprofit," and the pursuit of profit synonymous with indifference, and even hostility, toward human concerns. Far too often, it is the profit-motivated "system" which is blamed by the unthinking for the oppressiveness of urban life, racial and sexual inequalities, even war. Or so the litany of the militant, self-styled spokesmen of the nonprofit community would have it. Such anger and bitterness, of course, is not without foundation. There is no escaping history, and ours as a nation is as much a record of man's exploitation at the hands of his fellowman, of the weak preyed upon, manipulated, and abused by the powerful, as it is a chronicle of incredible technological achievement, and social and political change. It is undeniable that, for better or worse, we have evolved to a place as a nation that no other people we know of has ever been before. But the price of our rush to get here has been a staggering willingness to sacrifice a few of our number for the progress of us all.

The vital human quality that keeps us from devouring one another altogether, however, also gave us the wisdom to build into our system a means of providing for its victims. We did, in effect, recognize ourselves for what we are, and sought to balance our barely civilized selves with a mechanism for human caring which is highly organized and designed to function on a massive social scale. To fuel that mechanism we conceived a self-imposed tithe, payable from the material gain that our profit-oriented system provides. And we call it philanthropy.

In other words, for whatever reasons, we have determined to use the profit system to pay for the care of those who cannot survive within it. That is an irony we all could savor were its consequences not so perilous for today's nonprofit organizations. For these organizations, sharing as they must the perspective of the victim, have come to reject the values of the very system which makes their existence possible, as well as necessary. Never, since the French Revolution, have so many babies been thrown out with so little bath water.

It is even more ironic that we are living in an age when the nonprofits are needed more than ever before. We have pursued progress with the blithe confidence that we were making things steadily better. But here we are, now, almost 200 years later, and so little seems better, and so much seems to be growing worse. We once assumed that our public institutions were the proper vehicles "to insure the common good" and "promote the public welfare." We soon recognized it was not to be so. For we learned our government is representative of all of our society, and when that society was impatient to get somewhere, whether or not a few of its members were prepared for or capable of making the trip, our elected officials were not going to be the ones who missed the bus.

Today, the very size of our nation and the tenacity and diversity of its problems make it practically impossible for the government to perform the social welfare functions written into its charter. First, it must take care of itself, a task that requires enormous resources, and then it responds to what it perceives to be the priorities of the nation as a whole. When the few dollars left over finally sift down to education, health, housing, transportation, and welfare, there is simply too little coming too late to do much real and lasting good. Too, the very size of our government mitigates against its moving quickly and intelligently to deal with the problems that come with burgeoning social change.

Thus, the task of performing these services—if they are to be performed at all—falls to the private sector. Much like the agricultural society of 150 years ago, today we must look to ourselves for aid and comfort in times of crisis. Unfortunately, our crises seem to be multiplying, and each time we think we have banked the fires of one social problem, the flames blaze anew elsewhere. (Witness environmental pollution and the energy crisis.) New growth, new technology create new problems, and make old wounds all the more obvious. We are caught in one of history's sobering crunches in which circumstance, fate, and our own failings conspire to bludgeon us to wakefulness. We are not yet wise enough to lay the past to rest, not yet strong enough to welcome future change without fear.

The dilemma of the nonprofit community is awesome, and in so many ways, that community is ill-prepared to confront it. Not infrequently, the nonprofit community, by the very nature of its breadth and diversity, appears to be its own worst enemy. The more militant end of the nonprofit spectrum, including the radical left, flies the ugly colors of violence and moral blackmail. At the other end of the spectrum, we glimpse the dark hues of the morally bankrupt, the outright fraud who preys on our generosity for his own gain.

In the middle, different, but no less self-destructive, forces are at work. We always have prided ourselves on being a nation of citizen-activists, ready to form a posse, fight wars, build schoolhouses and churches at the slightest provocations. Today we may well ask ourselves what we have wrought. We are experiencing an unparalleled growth of organizations and institutions within the nonprofit community, and it has become axiomatic that wherever two people with a grievance gather together, there also you will find a new nonprofit group.

We appear to be approaching an imbalance in which our activist organizations outnumber the problems to be solved. Environmental and conservation organizations have sprung up so rapidly and in such great numbers that they now are engaged in sometimes bitter battles to carve out their own little pieces of the planet to save and to guard jealously against the encroaching concern of competing organizations. The growth of organizations to promote racial and sexual equality is racing ahead of the birthrate, and the number of new groups in housing, employment, and urban planning cannot be counted on all the fingers of all the members of all the committees which formed them.

This is not to deride the causes which these organizations espouse. But this nonprofit population explosion has led to duplication and inefficiency, which in turn breeds confusion, impotence, and futility. Many young groups are poorly structured at their inception, if they are structured at all, and principles of organization, goalsetting, finance, even common sense, are sacrificed in the heat generated by the immediacy of a problem to be solved. Such organizations are doomed to founder at the start. They have rushed recklessly into the social activist fray as if convinced that commitment, and an appropriate amount of noise, will bring them success.

The older, better established members of the nonprofit community are faring little better. We have only to look at private education in this country to discover—if we didn't know it already—that longevity is no guarantee of survival. Higher education, which we have elevated to a God-given right from its former status as a privilege, is in serious trouble. Institutions are closing their doors, giving up not by choice, but because of economic necessity. Our colleges and universities are awash in a sea of red ink, pushed under by growing public indifference not only to their plight, but to formal education itself. The corollary of the Puritan ethic that each of us must get a college education and make something of ourselves today seems to be little more than an amusing relic of a distant past for many of our young people. And their parents are too occupied with other concerns, perhaps simply too tired, to argue the point. The pressure is on.

Other familiar institutions in the middle of the nonprofit spectrum are equally troubled. We hear rumblings of gross mismanagement from among our long-respected, most prestigious health organizations. Leadership of nonprofit institutions increasingly has become merely a reward for the politically faithful. Social service organizations are finding themselves lost in the maze of their own bureaucracy, barely able to find the needy who require their services at the other end.

Everywhere there is anger. There is anger at the government for its stinginess in dealing with social problems. There is anger at the general public for its indifference. There is anger at ourselves among those of us who labor in the nonprofit vineyard because we seem to be accomplishing so little in a world that cries out for so much to be done. Above all else, there is outrage at a political and economic system which can be at once so remarkable and so flawed, that is responsible, many believe, for our being in this predicament in the first place. There is rage, and rejection.

And that brings the paradox of contemporary philanthropy full circle. Our nonprofit community no longer sees that it is in fact but another face of the profit system. Increasingly, expediency and alarm are leading us to reject not only the darker side of this system, but also the total system itself, and the values which have made it work. We have reached the point where we are saying, in deed if not so much in word, that if a system which values good bookkeeping also can tolerate poverty and ignorance, then we'll do without good bookkeeping. If the profit motive which inspires the best principles of sound management also inspires manipulation of the powerless, then let us pass on sound management. For after all, this reasoning goes, our cause is righteous, our motives are the best, and what does it matter if the books don't balance?

Well, what does it matter whether you survive? What's the difference if the problems of the nonprofit marketplace worsen, and one by one our institutions grow sleepy, senile, and die? What does it matter if we are unable to meet the new challenges which are being thrust upon us, and our scales, never quite in balance even at their best, collapse under the heavy weight of the drive for self-preservation that is in us all? What then the price of righteous indignation?

There is more than a little evidence to suggest that our entire system, and its nonprofit components, is entering a new era of profound change. Many believe that the upheavals we are experiencing now are far more than the fitful jolts and starts that distinguish day-to-day human development. Rather, we are about to be wrenched out of our familiar world and into a full-blown Age, one which will take its place in history right along side Dark, Reason, Renaissance, Industrialization, and Space. In other words, The Real McCoy in the chronicle of civilizations.

If there is even a modicum of truth in such speculation, our nonprofit institutions are going to play more vital a role than ever before. They are more than a convenient way to assuage feelings of guilt brought on by social self-indulgence. They are the repository of all that we deem the best in us, not only materially, but also spiritually as well. It may well be that our survival as a people—if not in physical fact, then at least in memory—will depend on them.

It is much more likely, of course, that change will come the way it usually does. It will sneak up on us while we are occupied elsewhere, a fleeting image on the screen of human existence that catches us out in the lobby, standing in line for popcorn. Change, as it almost always has, will seem to offer us more of the same, while slipping in a little something new to keep us on our toes.

But however change occurs, it is putting new pressures on and making new demands of our nonprofit organizations. As the need for the kinds of services only they can provide increases, nonprofits must come to grips with the system of which they are inextricably a part. They must abandon their aloof disdain for practical concerns of administrative and financial management. For if they are to be effective, they must first survive. And to survive, they must come to understand, and learn how to use, the values of the system which created them, and keeps them in business.

In fact, in many ways they must be better at the game than those who invented it. They must become goal-oriented and learn the art of creating and implementing programs that achieve them. Confronted with shortages in funds and manpower, they must develop finely-honed organizational skills that will enable them to use their limited resources for the greatest benefit. And our nonprofit institutions must learn the craft of salesmanship, and they must use it with the most sophisticated marketing tools at their command to ensure that the rest of the system better understands, and more generously supports, their work.

The nonprofit side of our total system cannot afford to detach itself from our society as a whole, to float off on a sea of self-congratulation. The role nonprofits have to play is far more significant than simply that of the ominously pointing finger. We have progressed just far enough so that the level of our society's expectations for the quality of life is rising steadily, and, more and more, it is to the nonprofit institutions that we turn to have these expectations fulfilled. In fact, the potential for the expansion of the role of the nonprofit is greater than ever before, and the nonprofit system is making inroads into what have been traditionally profit-oriented enterprises (broadcasting, transportation, housing).

No one knows for sure at what point it became clear that humanity could progress farther and faster by uniting and utilizing all of its resources, rather than remaining fragmented and therefore vulnerable. But it is basically the same reasoning that has led to the rise of philanthropy in this society, and the emergence of nonprofit enterprise as a fundamental component of our growth. If the nonprofit segment is to continue to play this vital role effectively, it must recognize and accept the capitalist blood flowing in its veins. Money and its management is no less of value to the doer of good deeds than it is to the seeker after profit.

It must be clear by now that it requires little skill or insight to be a Jeremiah in the land of the nonprofits. Jeremiah had only to answer to God. The nonprofits must answer to a board of directors, the Internal Revenue Service, and an increasingly vocal public who wants to know what's happening to the $25 billion it is spending for good works.

Jeremiah also had good material to work with in finding ways to stave off disaster. The word, after all, was coming straight from The Top. That is still a good source, but there are other answers, closer to earth, which also offer hope for the health and growth of our nonprofit community.

This book explores some of them.

2 EFFECTIVE ORGANIZATION... OR, HOW CAN YOU SEND A GREAT CAUSE UP IN A CRATE LIKE THAT?

Effective management of the nonprofit dollar begins with effective organization. From a moral point of view, the nonprofit segment of our social and economic system is charged with the protection and care of those who, for whatever reasons, cannot function competitively in a capitalist society. In baser terms, the nonprofit community is concerned chiefly with the manipulation of resources. More precisely, nonprofits seek to redirect spending from the pursuit of self-serving individual goals to the expenditure of resources in the service of goals which benefit the human welfare of society as a whole.

This is a task which requires the utmost care in its organization, especially in a society where there is constant tension between profit and nonprofit motives. Not only must great care be exercised in organizing the total system for the balanced distribution of resources, but also equal concern for organization must be shown by the individual components which make this process work. If nonprofit organizations and institutions are to function effectively, they must be as much concerned with the way in which the are structured and managed as those motivated by profit.

The key factor in effective organization is the identification and definition of goals. It is here that historically the greatest differences have existed between the profit and nonprofit segments of our system. It also is here that the fallout from the antiprofit mentality has had its most damaging effect on the efficient operation of nonprofit institutions.

In a society such as ours, no single organization or institution can responsibly claim to serve the needs of everyone. The nonprofit community, therefore, is segmented, as society is. As problems and issues have been identified or brought to public attention, organizations and institutions have been created to deal with them. At this level, there is a parallel between the nonprofit sector and the profit system, which itself evolved as businesses and industries formed or expanded to meet specific needs within our society.

But it is at the point of defining and implementing goals that this parallel ends. Profit-making organizations must clearly define their goals in a way that provides for their implementation. A business determines not only that it will make watches, but that it will make self-winding watches with leather bands that sell for $24.95, cost $4.50 to produce and distribute, and wear out in one year and three months. Once this goal is defined, the structure of that business is defined, and it will be organized and managed to implement that goal by producing its watches at a minimum cost and a maximum profit.

Nonprofit organizations, on the other hand, have held themselves to be above the considerations of the profit motive. Their goals generally are based not on such specific aims, but on broad philosophical concepts—justice, equality, brotherhood, human dignity, preservation of the environment. Only rarely, if at all, do such goals also incorporate an awareness of the need for mechanisms for their implementation. It is one thing for an organization to adopt the goal of preservation of the environment. It it quite a different thing for the same organization to adopt the goal of preserving the environment through legal action against those who pollute it. The latter goal encompasses a specific course of action for its implementation, or an "objective," which in turn dictates the kind of structure or organization required if it is to be attained. The former goal, on the other hand, is merely rhetoric.

The interrelatedness of goal setting and organization can be seen clearly in a brief comparison of the peace and civil rights movements of the 1960s. The civil rights movement enjoyed centralized and unified leadership. Its goals were based on a philosophical concept—racial equality—but also were defined to incorporate specific actions or events which in themselves determined how the movement was organized and these goals implemented. In contrast, the peace movement, with its decentralized leadership of varying political and social commitments, had as its goal a slogan: "End the war now." This was a goal whose philosophy was sound, but which was so poorly defined that it offered no clue to its implementation, nor to the kind of structure that would enhance its achievement.

The civil rights movement also related its goals to aspects of our society which—no matter how grudgingly—were susceptible to change. By defining one of its goals as equality within the political system, it followed that the movement organize itself to gain access to that system. It implemented a campaign to register voters who previously had been denied that right because of their race, and to elect candidates sympathetic to or representative of its point of view. The goal of political equality was one which also recognized that the system itself must respond to millions of new voters, moral issues aside. No members of Congress facing reelection could fail to see the benefits of yielding in some measure to this new political force.

Other goals of the civil rights movement shared similar characteristics. Economic equality was defined to include an end to discrimination in hiring and advancement policies in both the public and the private sectors. Social equality encompassed the elimination of racial discrimination in housing, transportation, and public facilities. In each case, goals were adopted as definite ends which required a specific structure and implementation for their attainment. And when advocates of racial equality sought to sway society at the moral level, their case was strengthened by real examples of the struggle of the movement to attain its goals. The cry of "racial discrimination" was not merely rhetoric, but demonstrable fact.

The advocates of an end to the war in Southeast Asia borrowed much of the rhetoric and style, but little else, of the civil rights movement. With its leadership pulled in many political directions at once, the peace movement was unable to define its goals in a way that would enhance organization of those sympathetic to its ends into an effective force for change. Essentially goalless, the peace movement resorted to sloganeering and attacks on personalities. As its rhetoric grew more heated, its effectiveness correspondingly diminished.

In addition, unlike the civil rights movement, the peace movement failed to relate its "goals" to the machinery of society which could be changed. It offered no real alternatives to the war, and no political leader whose constituency depended upon the defense establishment for its livelihood could advocate dismantling that establishment, as the peace movement came to demand. Even the rhetorical demand—as opposed to a goal—of "self-determination for the people of South Vietnam" was a practical impossibility, short of the use of force by the United States government.

This comparison is not to suggest that either movement was more or less just or worthy. Nor does it justify an inference that one was a total success and the other a total failure. It does suggest that, because of the way in which it defined its goals, the civil rights movement realized a measure of achievement that the peace movement could not. The history of the two movements underscores the relationship of goal setting and effective organization. It cannot be stressed too strongly that how an institution defines its goals is, in the final analysis, as important to its success as its goals themselves.

But obviously, the survival and effectiveness of nonprofits is more than a matter of proper goal setting. The structure which sound goals dictate itself is made up of many different elements, and the role of each must be clearly understood and its function defined if an organization or institution is to succeed in its mission, prosper financially, and grow.

The structural elements of nonprofit organizations are so well known as to be taken for granted. We all know that to run an institution or organization you must have a board of directors, an executive officer, and a staff. But what is it that a board of directors actually does? What are the responsibilities of the executive officer, and where does the staff fit into the total organizational picture? Despite what we may like to think we know about each of the organizational elements, there is a great deal of evidence in the nonprofit community to indicate that each is subject to common misconceptions about its function and importance which, like improperly defined goals, result in nonprofits performing in ways that are not only inefficient, but also irresponsible.

Many nonprofits seem to "happen" rather than to develop logically along well-planned paths related to the achievement of their goals. Most often such unplanned and poorly thought out organization masquerades as program expansion or improvement of services, or even as increased efficiency. However it occurs, its effect on nonprofits is disastrous, robbing them of vital energy and resources, and creating organizational confusion which carries them farther and farther from their goals.

To better understand how such errors in growth and management occur, and how they can affect an organization let's take a look at one of the oldest and largest associations in the nonprofit community The National Association for the Treatment and Prevention of Malocclusion—known commonly as the Overbite Fund—was founded more than 40 years ago. Its goal then as now is "the eradication of malformation of human teeth through research and public education." From what we know of goal setting, already we can appreciate that the Fund is in trouble.

Today the Fund has 125 employees who occupy two floors of a new high-rise office building in the suburbs of Washington, D.C. It has a 65-member board of directors which meets twice a year—once to approve whatever recommendations the staff makes to them, and once at the annual convention to sit on its dais. As the health field grew more specialized, the Fund expanded to comprise seven branches, each itself a national association of professionals ranging from speech therapists to educational psychologists. Each branch has its own goals, by-laws, and qualifications for membership, and each is represented on the board.

Management of the Fund is in the hands of the executive director, a former Public Health Service officer whose responsibility was contract review. He is assisted by three deputy directors, and seven program administrators, each of whom also serves as executive secretary of one of the association's seven branch organizations. The Fund maintains five regional offices throughout the nation, the better to carry on its public education function at the local level. The program administrators' chief function is to generate programs. Proposals are in the works to seek foundation funding for research and education projects on malocclusion and the energy crisis, and for a comparative study of the effects of overbite on the cultural adjustment of disadvantaged preschool children among racial minorities in seven major urban centers.

In addition, the program administrators are responsible for the production of one weekly, three monthly, four quarterly, two biannual, and three annual publications. They also produce guidelines and informational materials for professionals in the field, and for Congress and federal administrative agencies concerned with legislation and regulations affecting malocclusion.

The research function of the association is carried on currently by two specialists just added to its staff. One is a Ph.D. in landscape gardening who is studying the effects of malocclusion on the environment, with federal funds. The other is an M.A. in elementary education who is researching the relationship between overbite and learning disabilities under a grant from a small foundation. At the moment, they are the center of a bitter internal struggle to determine whom they will report to within the organizational structure.

The Overbite Fund has an annual budget of $4.5 million. This year it will generate a deficit of $500,000. The board with few exceptions has made it clear that its job is to decide questions of policy, and has given the executive director the responsibility of raising money. The executive director, of course, is overburdened with the day-to-day administration of the association. The program administrators are generating programs, and the researchers are researching. The association's last fund-raising effort cost $32,500 to mount, and netted $132.50. Major foundations no longer seem interested in programs in "research and public education." No one knows where the money is coming from to cover this year's deficit.

The Overbite Fund is, of course, fictitious. But the structure described here, and the problems inherent in it, are factual and based on a very real organization that is functioning today. Even more sobering, our fictional Fund is typical of thousands of organizations and institutions in the middle range of the nonprofit community. Poorly defined goals aside, this organization demonstrates a fundamental ignorance of what a board of directors is and what it is that it does. Nor is it any clearer in its conceptualization of the roles and responsibilities of its executive director and staff.

Such chaos need not occur. To understand more fully the alternatives to such disorder, let us examine in the remainder of this chapter each of the elements of the nonprofit organization at length, always keeping in mind the primary function of the nonprofit community—the sound management of resources. Later we will explore how these elements are combined in an effective and effectively managed organization.

THE BOARD OF DIRECTORS

The board of directors of an organization or institution has serious responsibilities far beyond window dressing which gives an air of credibility. The board, in legal fact, *is* the organization, and the stewardship of cash and other assets of the organization resides in it. An organization's status under federal tax laws, the purchase or sale of property, its power to bring legal action in the courts—and its vulnerability to lawsuits—in fact, the very authority to create or dismantle itself all rests with its board of directors.

Thus, a board is more than a "paper tiger," and its responsibilities must be taken seriously. For example, the Internal Revenue Service recently revoked an organization's tax exemption (under Section 501(c)(3) of the Tax Code) on the grounds that several members of the board of a commercial firm also sat on the board of the nonprofit. IRS held that the nonprofit was in fact controlled by the commercial firm, and was being used by it unlawfully to evade taxation. The nonprofit won the first round in the courts, but, as of this writing, IRS has not decided whether to appeal that decision. The point is that increasingly the structure of nonprofits is coming under scrutiny by the federal government, and nonprofit organizations would be wise to determine now whether the composition and function of their boards can withstand close examination.

In the profit sector of our economy, membership on boards of directors is usually based on sound business reasons. Individuals are elected to boards—or asked to participate in their formation—because they possess skills or experience otherwise unavailable to a corporation, or because they have invested substantial enough sums of money in it to have a voice in how it is managed. If David Rockefeller is on the board of the Smertz Screw Co., he is there because Chase Manhattan Bank owns a sizeable portion of the company's stock. He was not asked to be there because the glamour of his family name might rub off on Smertz Screws. Equally important, the boards of profit-motivated businesses generally are well-organized to perform specific duties related to management of those businesses. They are structured to make key decisions about expansion, acquisition of new properties, capitalization. They may delegate responsibility for implementation of those decisions, but not the authority to make them.

There is much that the nonprofit corporation may learn from the example of the profit-motivated corporation. The nonprofit board must be created to perform specific functions, not merely to lend its name to a good cause. The nonprofit organization must have written into its charter board authority to make decisions and to delegate responsibilities. Every board member must be made to understand that he or she is there because that individual possesses a skill that is vital to the successful operation of the organization. The board itself must be structured so that these skills are put to work, and the board becomes a complement to the staff of the organization, as well as its overseer.

Far too often, nonprofit boards are created solely to provide an organization with weight it believes it otherwise would lack. This most often happens in organizations whose goals and performance give good reason to doubt their seriousness of purpose and effectiveness. The organization usually looks for a couple of businessmen to demonstrate its solidity, a politician or two for visibility, a black or a woman or both to prove it is democratic, an educator to show its seriousness of purpose, and a clergyman for spirituality. In short, it seeks credence and representativeness when it should be seeking efficient management.

This approach to organization of a board also is symptomatic of most nonprofits' attitudes toward raising money. Prospective board members are courted on the basis of their ties to sources of funds—real or imagined—rather than their proven abilities as fund-raisers. Nonprofits tend to assume that certain board members have access to funds otherwise unavailable to them simply because they are representative of or have relationship with monied individuals or groups within the profit sector. Such board members are selected for the money which they may be able to attract, rather than for the funds they themselves can contribute directly and can wring from potential sources of money.

This is one of the most serious shortcomings of this approach to board organization. It is likely that the businessman looks to his participation as a matter of status which elevates him above his less civic-minded colleagues. The politician has his own worries, not the least of which is raising money for his next campaign. Minority representatives usually come to a board already committed to other organizations aligned with their personal concerns. The educator is looking for funds for his next research project or to buy him the time to write his next book. And as for the clergyman, well, to be perfectly blunt, what can you expect from someone who has to pass the hat once a week for his own sustenance?

The fact of the matter is that the first responsibility of a board is to raise money. There will be no organization to direct unless they perform this function successfully, and it is one that cannot be left to chance. The primary criterion for board membership must be the direct contribution of funds. The contribution of services, while highly important, is secondary. Personal contributions of money by board members is not only a very real measure of their commitment to a cause, but also the only supportable basis for their asking for money from others. No individual, corporation, or foundation is going to give money to an organization which cannot convince its own board of directors to contribute monetarily to its financial development.

The most effective nonprofit boards are those which—once they have fulfilled their financial responsibilities—are organized to provide guidance and management in specific areas of an organization's operation. In substance, generally, these areas are administration, program, and finance, and the board's membership is structured into committees to deal with matters of policy and procedure affecting each. It is the board's responsibility to decide how an organization will be managed and who will do it, what programs it will undertake, and where its money will come from and how it will be spent. As is the case in the profit sector, the responsibility for implementing the board's decisions in each of these areas may be delegated to others, but the authority to make such decisions cannot be if the organization is to be effective.

When a board abdicates or is denied the power to make these decisions, the organization suffers accordingly. For all the duties and responsibilities of a board are related directly to the definition and implementation of goals. The board is the pivotal point upon which the attainment of an organization's goals turns. It is the board that determines what an organization's goals will be, and when and how they will be refined to meet the changing needs of society over time. If the board is strong, positively motivated, and properly structured it will instill these qualities in the organization it represents and that organization will succeed. If a board is weak, indifferent to or ignorant of its purpose, and without structure, the organization will fail.

A board of directors does not exist because all organizations must have one, or because a certain list of names makes an organization look good. A board has an absolutely essential role to play, and nothing can substitute for it in determining the success of a nonprofit organization.

THE EXECUTIVE DIRECTOR

If the importance of goal setting and the role of the board stand at the top of the hierarchy of misconceptions in the nonprofit marketplace, the role of the executive director is next in line. The executive director most often is expected to be a super administrator, fund raiser, diplomat, legislative specialist, and program coordinator, as well as knowledgeable and experienced in whatever field his organization labors.

Where the board is weak and ineffective, he is expected to make and to implement decisions that are not his responsibility, and may well be beyond his competence. Where the board is strong, or dominated by a few strong personalities, he is expected to be a middle man who passes the board's orders on to the staff and reports back on the staff's progress and performance in carrying them out. At the same time, it is usually he who is held responsible for the success or failure of the organization, and his career may rise or fall on the caprice of forces over which he has no control.

In discussing his role, the executive director of a major nonprofit organization said recently: "I don't really know what this place needs me for. The board doesn't want an executive director, it wants a messenger boy. We've got some very important people on our board, some very impressive names. They don't really do anything, but they've got my staff completely cowed. My people are more concerned about upsetting the board than they are about doing their job. My comptroller is more afraid of (a board member) than he is of our losing money. Every time we have to make a decision, somebody pops up and asks, 'Well, what is so-and-so going to think?' When you get right down to it, I'm a manager with nothing to manage."

The other side of the organizational coin was revealed during what might be called an informal dialogue, in a hotel cocktail lounge, with the executive of a major educational institution. His observation: "I'll tell you the truth. I don't think my board could care less what's going on at (our institution). The only time I see three-quarters of them is during the annual meeting, and the rest only show up when they want something. In the past three years they've contributed exactly $11,233. I have to make all the decisions, and, let's face it, as smart as I am I don't know everything. There are times when some of these people—say a guy whose built a multimillion dollar business—could be damned helpful. But you try and find them when you really need them.

"And it's gotten to the point where nobody really cares whether we do our job or not. Sometimes I think we could get away with anything. Oh, the board will say no to something every now and then just to show they can if they want to. But most of the time, they just say okay to whatever we tell them. Now a lot of people in my place would think that's terrific. But I'm telling you this can't go on forever. It's all going to catch up with us one day. And when it does, it's going to be yours truly who gets it right in the . . ."

Both of these men—decently motivated and reasonably competent—are victims of the misunderstanding and misuse of the executive director that is found throughout the nonprofit community. The executive director fundamentally plays a role that is no different than that of the key administrator of an organization in the profit sector. Both are responsible for the maximum utilization of their organizations' resources, at a minimum cost, to produce a product at a profit. In the nonprofit sector, the product is programs or services, rather than goods, and the profit is the benefit or betterment of all or a portion of society. But the responsibility of both is basically the same—effective management.

One of the most common errors in the operation of nonprofit organizations is the blurring of the management and performance functions.

Often the executive director is expected to perform the tasks he is charged with managing, which is much like expecting the vice president for production of a major automobile manufacturer also to spend his time on the assembly line, putting his company's cars together. Thus, while the executive director is responsible for the management of the nonprofit's fundraising function, for example, he cannot also be held responsible for the performance of that function. To demand of him that he do both is to weaken the effectiveness of the organization in each area. Similarly, the executive director cannot manage the program or service function of an organization if he himself is expected to generate and implement those programs or services.

It is important that the management role of the executive director be clearly understood. It is his task to translate the decisions of the board on goals, organization, and policy into day-to-day realities. His function is to see that each element of his organization fully comprehends its task and carries it out effectively and economically. He is responsible for pulling together each of these elements into a cohesive structure which successfully implements the organization's objectives. He is the manager of the organization's resources—human and financial—in the service of its goals.

To do his job, he must have the proper guidance and support from his board, and he must have access to adequate resources within the organization itself. It is not enough that the board play out its decision-making role and simply abandon the implementation of those decisions to the executive director. The board must also see that the executive director has the authority to carry out his assigned task, and that it is to him, and not to the board, that the organization's staff looks for its leadership.

By the same token, the executive director has certain responsibilities to the board of directors. It is his responsibility to keep the board informed of the organization's progress toward its goals, and to identify problems or issues for the board which require their action. He must be sure that the board is aware of the organization's achievements and problems, and that the board understands clearly the source of the organization's funds, and the rationale for its spending practices. The executive director, where he can, must provide guidance for the board to help it meet its responsibilities effectively.

In essence, the relationship between the board and the executive director is a symbiotic one. The executive director is the mechanism through which the board of directors realizes its aims, and the board, for its part, functions to guide and nurture the executive director in the performance of his duties. When this relationship is in balance, an organization or institution is healthy and will prosper. When executive director and board become adversaries through the failure of either to understand and perform their duties responsibly, the organization will become ineffective, wither, and die.

THE STAFF

The role of the staff in the effective nonprofit organization is in many ways the most difficult to define because it is seemingly so obvious. In the simplest terms, the staff is the front-line troops, the men and women who on a daily basis do the work that is necessary to implement the goals of an organization or institution. Their function often is taken for granted, yet their role is in one sense the most sensitive of any element of an organization.

One of the most prevalent problems in the nonprofit community is the failure to properly define staff functions. A veteran of the nonprofit marketplace once remarked that, while an employee of the nation's largest doer of good deeds, the part of his job he dreaded most was that time each year when he was called upon to describe his function and to offer his evaluation of how well he was doing it. "I realized," he said, that while I knew perfectly well how good I was at what I was doing, I really had no idea of what it was that I was good at.

It is at the staff level that goals and their implementation get translated into specific deeds, and that is no simple task. It requires a clear understanding of what it is that an organization seeks to accomplish, and the most effective means of accomplishing it. Unlike the board, and to a lesser degree the executive director, the staff does not deal in the gross generalities of an organization, but rather performs specialized tasks within it. These tasks taken individually may be more or less significant to overall goals, but taken together they determine whether or not the job gets done at all. This problem is compounded by the fact that nonprofits, like any organization in society, must carry on both housekeeping functions to ensure that they run smoothly internally, and "product" functions that determine their performance in the marketplace externally.

These functions should be clearly separated, and, wherever possible, the staff responsible for internal duties should not also be given responsibility for an organization's product. There are, of course, points where these two broader functions overlap, most generally in the area of financial management. But aside from keeping the books, those organizations perform most effectively in which the duties of their personnel are precisely defined, and their roles in the larger scheme of things are carefully spelled out. The staff must be recognized as a key element in the total organization, and it must be understood that its specialized tasks taken together determine—as much as the definition of goals, the performance of the board and of the executive director—the success or failure of an organization.

3 EFFECTIVE ORGANIZATION II... OR, BEGINNING TO PUT ALL THE PIECES TOGETHER

So far, we have discussed four fundamental elements of nonprofit management: goal setting, the board of directors, the executive officer, and the staff. Obviously these elements do not exist in a vacuum; each interrelates with the others at many different levels, with varying impact on the realization of goals and the ultimate success or failure of an institution. It is more than the pursuit of commonly held goals which cements the structure of an institution together. While goals must be defined in a way which suggests structure and implementation, the way in which the components of that structure interact also determines an organization's effectiveness.

Organizational structure is more than neatly drawn lines on paper and the precise arrangement of titles and functions in an ascending pyramid. Structure is a living thing that shifts and changes over the life of an organization. It is people, programs, and procedures which make up an institution's structure. As these are nurtured and developed, and grow stronger and more efficient, the institution, too, improves and performs more effectively. Where people, programs, and procedures are permitted to stagnate, become taken for granted, even ignored, the underpinnings of an institution begin to decay, and it eventually will start to crumble from within.

One of the barriers to the development of a strong institutional structure is the human tendency to equate the naming of things with their doing. We tend to believe that by finding a name for a disease, we are on the road to recovery from its effects. We see this almost daily in our federal government. The President announces with pious solemnity that another major problem has been brought under control with the formation of an impressively and appropriately labeled agency or commission. We see it closer to home in the reaction of city governments to social upheavals among minorities. Here the response most often has been not to attack the causes of the problems, but rather to create new agencies or councils which is a political form of sleight-of-hand that substitutes for action.

Nonprofit organizations are no less inclined to play this form of the old shell game. Experience in the nonprofit community indicates that organizations and institutions spend as much time creating titles and labels as they do performing their functions. It is this mentality which, in terms of structure, equates the naming of a deputy director for administration, for example, with efficient management of the institution, or the announcement of the creation of a program on drug abuse with solution of the problem. It is almost axiomatic that the more complex an issue, the greater the amount of time and energy that will be spent in giving it a name, and the less devoted to practicalities of its resolution.

The deadening effect of this game on the performance of an organization cannot be overly emphasized. First, it robs people within the organization of real and meaningful labor, which produces an adverse effect on their attitudes toward themselves, their jobs, and the goals of the organization itself. Second, it encourages the proliferation of bureaucracy, which disperses energy and resources that most institutions can ill afford to waste. And third, it diverts an organization from its goals, and over time renders it, for all practical purposes, useless.

People and procedure are the nonprofit's most effective weapons in overcoming the naming-as-doing syndrome. As noted earlier, it is people who make realities of the goals of an organization. They perform most effectively when their jobs are clearly defined and they have some sense of being intimately involved in the service of a larger purpose. But no matter how effective individual staff members may be, their contributions must be viewed within the context of a total mechanism which gives their efforts cohesion and direction. Procedure, the dictionary tells us, is the "act of proceeding in any action or process; a particular course or mode of action." Procedure to the nonprofit is the organized plan for performance that makes possible the implementation of its goals.

The issues of program are complex enough to require a chapter to themselves. It is important here to make the distinction between program and procedure. Program is the external manifestation of an organization's goals, the point at which the organization intersects with its public. Procedure is an internal mechanism, the path along which performance moves a program or service from conception to public implementation.

Nonprofits tend to concentrate on program to the detriment of procedure. It is far easier for the improperly managed nonprofit to focus on problems in the society at large, than it is to turn its attention inwardly on itself and its own shortcomings. But if the nonprofit is chaotic and ineffective within, its programs will be chaotic and ineffectual. Structure in terms of program is not synonymous with the structure of an organization, and no matter how ambitious programs individually cannot substitute for the procedures that are necessary to a well-structured and efficiently operated organization.

Because it is people who create and make procedures work, it is logical that our discussion of the role of both in effective management begin with them. There is a very important rule in the management of people within any organization—profit and nonprofit—that is so rudimentary that one is almost embarrassed to mention it here. Yet it is a rule that is overlooked with surprising frequency in the nonprofit community. This is the fundamental law of performance which states that people should be qualified for the jobs they hold, and properly trained to do them.

Managerial responsibility in the nonprofit institution too often has become a reward for services rendered elsewhere. On the campus, for example, the professor who has ambitions to rise within the institutional hierarchy must give up what he does best, and has been educated to do, to assume an administrative post for which he has had little or no training and no real experience. A scientist who sees no room at the top in the profit-oriented corporation for which he works may end his career as a program administrator in a professional association, a leap of some magnitude from the laboratory. It is not surprising to find a politician, whose constituency has had a change of heart about his usefulness, directing the affairs of a nonprofit organization. There is at least one major foundation in this country that has developed a reputation as a haven for non-elected government officials, sub-cabinet administrators, and White House aides between jobs.

There is no logic to dictate that, because he has been around long enough to grasp how an institution works, a college professor is qualified to play a role in running it. Nor is the scientific method so readily adaptable to the management and administration of a nonprofit organization that it can be assumed that the successful, or at least dedicated, scientist will be equally productive in such a new role. And our nonprofit foundations and organizations surely realize that the skills of maneuvering in the service of political power are not the most valuable tools which they can borrow from the profit sector to improve their own management.

The organizations and institutions of the nonprofit community face serious staffing problems. They generally cannot offer the salaries or benefits of the profit sector, such as profit-sharing and stock options. In the medium-sized organization or institution there is usually little opportunity for advancement upward, and professional movement is most often lateral, from organization to organization. In addition, there is no real training ground for administrative careers in the nonprofit sector. While some organizations and educational institutions may offer limited seminars or workshops in nonprofit management, there are few if any colleges or universities which offer such training in their curricula. Aside from volunteer service, the portals through which individuals may enter management careers in the nonprofit community are few in number, and exceedingly narrow.

This situation arises from a variation of the familiar law of supply and demand on a social scale. Because, by and large, we do not recognize the nonprofit sector for what it is—the other side of the profit-motivated coin and an essential element of our economy—we do not encourage our young to seek careers within it. In childhood, we are not inclined to play vice president for development meets foundation administrator, or disadvantaged minority confronts program coordinator. Our films, rightfully called the reflection of our dreams for ourselves and our society, feature heroes who ride tall in the saddle, not in the wing-backed executive chair. There are no manufactured children's games called "Staff Conference," "Direct Mail Appeal," or "Annual Convention" (although there are those who claim that the latter is just a grown-up version of that perennial childhood favorite, "Doctor"). Whatever it is Barbie and Ken do for a living, it certainly is not related to the nonprofit motive.

Thus, we have no childhood models for the nonprofit community, as we do for the profit sector, which we are urged to look to, admire, and emulate. Our public schools and institutions of higher education function to aid and abet the profit system. While we may be encouraged to enter careers of "public service"—doctor, nurse, teacher—the nonprofit segment generally is ignored, both as a functioning and relevant part of our society, and as a marketplace in which to pursue careers of significance. Since there is no encouragement, and thus no demand, to enter the nonprofit field, there is no adequate supply of trained and qualified personnel.

As a result, nonprofit organizations and institutions pretty much have to take their staffs where they can find them. The professor, the scientist, the politician, all find their way into the nonprofit institution because, in the worse sense, often they are the only persons qualified for it. They know just enough about a great deal in general, and little enough about what they are getting into, to be prime candidates for management posts in the nonprofit sector.

Often, of course, things do work out well. There are among the administrators of our nonprofit institutions highly qualified, able, and knowledgeable persons who perform difficult jobs admirably. But these administrators have learned their craft at the hands of the cruelest teacher—experience. When the financial stability of an institution or the effectiveness of its programs hang on a single decision, as they sometimes do, experience indeed can be a hard and expensive way to learn the business of nonprofit management.

The nonprofit community must begin to re-educate society so that our collective vision of its role and its relationship to the profit sector is cleared. To do so, that community itself must first recognize and accept its kinship with the profit-motivated aspects of our system. The nonprofit sector must insist that it is incorporated into our educational system just as other segments of our society are, that our young people are encouraged—or at least offered the opportunity to explore— careers in the nonprofit "industry," and that the higher education and training necessary for such careers is made available.

These are clearly long-range goals for improving the quality of management in the nonprofit marketplace. What of the here and now? What can the nonprofit institution do today to strengthen its human resources?

To begin with, an organization must identify the number, kinds, and functions of persons it requires to perform effectively. These decisions are primarily elements of organization and structure, and will be explored later in this chapter. But for the purposes of our discussion here, it should be stressed that such decisions must be formalized and written into the institution's structural definition of itself. The number and roles of persons within an organization naturally will change as that organization grows or adapts itself to new needs it identifies as falling within the scope of its purposes. Such changes can occur smoothly and efficiently, however, only when there is a clear understanding of their basis. To get from "here" to "there" an organization must have some comprehension of the points from which change or growth begin. Implicit in this process is the need for regular review of nonprofit personnel to determine that those functions which have been defined are in fact being performed. This review helps to determine those tasks for which a need no longer exists, and which can be considered completed and discarded from the organization's structural definition. At the same time, this exercise also identifies new tasks which may have sprung up but are not clearly defined, or which may be in the process of emerging and in need of being fulfilled.

The tasks of the nonprofit, like those of its profit-motivated counterpart, must be goal-oriented. Obviously the goals of an organization or institution are best served when these tasks are performed by people who are qualified to do them. The nonprofit generally has two sources for its personnel. It may seduce them away from other organizations in the nonprofit or profit sectors, and it may develop them from within. The effective nonprofit is organized to do both. If an organization recognizes that it has much to learn from the profit sector, it will make a concerted effort to attract to its ranks those people who have experience and a record of performance in it. The manager who has learned his craft well in the profit marketplace will certainly strengthen the nonprofit institution, bringing to it skills and knowledge that most organizations sorely need but rarely can secure within their own ranks.

Nonprofits must begin to provide more effectively for the growth of personnel within their own marketplace. The responsibility of managers is to manage, to direct the labor of others. Nonprofit managers frequently have not learned to share responsibility with those who labor at the staff level. Yet staff must be encouraged to participate in management decisions, and not merely relegated to implementing them, if they are to grow and become increasingly valuable to the organization over time. Provision must be made within an organization for its personnel to play even-broader roles in its management. For if vertical advancement is limited because of an organization's size, then the only alternative—in addition to remuneration—is "promotion" through expanded responsibilities.

The effects of this policy can have far-reaching significance for an organization or institution. The more responsibility a manager's staff assumes or is delegated the more time he is free to manage, to weigh and make decisions, create new programs or procedures which affect the organization's growth and effectiveness. At the same time, staff members themselves feel a deeper involvement in the institution and the attainment of its goals, and their satisfaction in experiencing meaningful results and recognition for their efforts enhances their productivity. An institution has good reason to fear for its health and effectiveness when it finds all decisions rest in the hands of a relative few. This is a symptom of poor management, inadequate staff, or both, and the results of the disease can be fatal.

In managing personnel effectively, an organization must be aware of its long-range objectives as well as the short-term necessities of getting the job done today. It must consider where its top management is coming from in five, ten, or twenty years. It should be sure that it can fill these posts from within with able and experienced individuals who fully comprehend the structure and function of an organization and the marketplace in which it operates. The alternative is the "revolving door" syndrome which results in time and energy being misdirected from sound management to the training and adjustment of new staff. For the average nonprofit, it is far more sensible from a management point of view to cultivate and to nurture leadership from within, than to be constantly in search of new personnel for whom the cycle of training and development must be begun anew.

For these reasons, it is imperative that the nonprofit develop in-service training programs. The object of such programs is not only to provide leadership for the future, but also to insure that management and staff are adequately equipped for their jobs in the here-and-now. In many middle-range nonprofits, training for the new employee is haphazard at best, and nonexistent for those who have been around for any period of time and are moving up the management ladder. Many organizations, both profit and nonprofit, make the dangerous assumption that length of service is in itself adequate training. But, it is likely that the longer the term of employment, the more ingrained the misconceptions about an organization's goals, the more fixed poor work habits, and the more rampant inefficiency becomes. In addition, frequently the in-service training which does take place is the responsibility solely of longer-term employees, thus perpetuating whatever shortcomings exist in the organization.

If it is to be effective, a training program must have some objective basis from which to begin. An employee cannot be trained properly unless the organization has some means of determining how much that employee already knows, the nature of the employee's attitudes about work in general, and about the work of the organization specifically. In this area, nonprofits must again look to their profit-motivated counterparts, and adapt skill and attitudinal testing to their own personnel development programs.

There is widespread distrust and disdain in the nonprofit community toward such testing. Nonprofit organizations and institutions, especially those working with sensitive social problems, tend to see in personnel testing a negative connotation which objectively it does not deserve. Nonprofit managers frequently view testing as computerized tyranny, an evil of standardization whose aim is to compartmentalize and dehumanize the individual. Testing, such managers are likely to tell you, is a device of the social scientist for making people fit categories and behavior patterns which the scientist already has defined. And, so another side of the anti-testing argument goes, there are some qualities of human beings which tests just can't measure, and it is those qualities that are often most important in the work that the nonprofit organization does. Besides—and this usually is offered as the clincher—employees themselves would never sit still for it.

It is true that there are many things which testing can and cannot do, but no one who understands and uses this tool claims that it is ultimately definitive in all things concerning human behavior. Whatever our personal feelings about ourselves and our human-ness, it is undeniable that there is a wide range of things about us that are observable, measurable, and therefore, to some extent, predictable. It is true that there are some qualities of human beings that cannot be measured—except under the most closely controlled circumstances—but it also is true that there are many qualities that can indeed be measured—intelligence, skills, reasoning ability, characteristics of leadership for example. It is extremely unlikely that those qualities which testing in popular use today cannot measure have anything at all to do with the management or service of a nonprofit organization. This excuse for not using tests, like that of potential employee revolt, is most often based on fear—the fear that if tested, an individual might be found wanting. Testing, properly used, however, does more than determine who is to survive and who is expendable. Its results point to how existing skills may be strengthened, misconceptions corrected, and efficiency improved. Personnel testing is a tool of management, not its dictator.

It is only after the skills and attitudes of new and existing employees have been determined that a nonprofit can begin to create effective in-service training programs. There can be little doubt that such programs are needed. Typically, a nonprofit employee's training consists of an introduction to the goals and programs of an organization, and to his or her niche in the organizational structure. The employee is introduced to co-workers, and provided all the memoranda and correspondence relevant to the job that can be dug out of the files. If the organization or institution considers itself really progressive, the employee may be led through a series of interviews with key managers "to get the big picture." After that, armed with data on pay days, sick leave and vacations, and health insurance, the new staffer is on his or her own.

But training also is another word for education, and education, we all know, is an on-going process. An effective training program does not only redirect the skills an employee already possesses to fill needs of an organization. It also provides for expanding and strengthening those skills. In-service training is more than an adaptive process; its primary function is educative. At any given point in the training process, an employee should know more and do it more effectively than he or she did upon first entering that process. The goal of the ideal in-service training program is not only to make file clerks better file clerks, but also—within the limitations of ambition and ability—to prepare file clerks to become program assistants, program assistants to become managers, managers to become vice presidents, and so on throughout the organization's structure. The most damning indictment of the absence or inefficiency of personnel development programs in the nonprofit sphere is the number of organizations and institutions which must go outside their own ranks for competent middle management and top leadership.

It also must be stressed that effective training encompasses new knowledge or techniques which emerge in a particular field of specialty. The scientist, manager, or technician in the profit sector is commonly expected to keep current on developing knowledge in his field. There is no reason why a nonprofit should demand any less of its own staff. An organization must provide whatever time and resources are necessary for the members of its staff to keep abreast of new developments which will affect their performance in their jobs. This is expecially true for the upper levels of management, where the assumption of knowledge may or may not be well founded, and where the opportunities for isolation from reality and ossification of misconceptions are the greatest. It is a serious error to assume that, because certain individuals have ascended to positions of responsibility, they can not benefit from additional training or education.

In summary, effective management of personnel in the nonprofit community, as in the profit-motivated sector of the society of which it is a part, begins with the clear definition of goal oriented tasks. Because nonprofit organizations and institutions operate under certain limitations not shared by the profit sector, they must show special concern for the advancement and training of their personnel. Where vertical advancement is restricted because of size or structure, personnel at the staff level must be encouraged to share in management, and their training must be an on-going process which enhances their involvement at this level, and which is designed to broaden their knowledge and improve their efficiency as they progress in the organization.

At first glance, effective personnel management may seem an expensive and time-consuming exercise requiring human and financial resources beyond the grasp of most medium-sized nonprofits. This need not be the case. Part of the effective manager's function is to develop personnel working under him so that they may assume increasingly greater portions of his duties and responsibilities. His value as a creative decision-maker is strengthened to the degree that the day-to-day functions of his office are performed well by others. In-service training itself need not be highly regimented or complex. It can be an evolving process in which staff at all levels grow in skills and knowledge together, interacting in shared learning experiences which create unity as well as efficiency. Such an approach makes it possible for a nonprofit to develop the leadership it requires from within, and thus increases the effectiveness of its management.

To this point we have confined ourselves to the issues and problems of the salaried staff in the nonprofit organization. We cannot overlook the very special questions which arise from the management of volunteer personnel. Volunteers are the backbone of the nonprofit sector. For it was the willingness of citizens to band together voluntarily to attack common problems which led to the institutionalization of philanthropy which we know today. But even though volunteers are utilized widely throughout the nonprofit community, attitudes about the work they do and how they are to be managed vary greatly.

Some organizations use volunteers simply because they believe they should have them around. Others have large, highly-trained, and tightly-disciplined volunteer staffs, without whom the work of the organization would not get done. There are nonprofits who recognize the importance of careful management of their volunteers, and there are those who are, in effect, victims of their volunteer staffs. And of course there is a broad range of organizations that could be using volunteers to increase their efficiency but are not doing so. There is no simple way to determine when and how volunteers may best be used within an organization, and their presence is often more a question of economics than anything else. It is certain, however, that the same principles of sound personnel management which are applied to paid staffs also must be exercised in dealing with the volunteer.

In terms of numbers alone, most volunteer participation is limited to a single activity, performed perhaps only once annually—door-to-door and street-corner collections for national charities, for example. In this instance, management of the volunteer staff is relatively simple. National headquarters and or local chapters organize neighborhood or block chairpersons who recruit their "staffs" to collect money that is then funnelled back to the national organization. By and large, the volunteer worker is then through until the next year. This is a simple and effective means of raising money for an organization, requiring little management of the volunteer participants. Usually volunteers are given a briefing by a local chapter representative, or just some literature to read, provided a can with a slot in the top, and sent out on the street with instructions on where to turn in the money. Unless the volunteer also performs some other function—driving handicapped children on outings, secretarial work on a part-time basis for small local chapters, stuffing envelopes—he or she has no role in shaping the programs and policies of an organization.

This use of volunteers also is extremely difficult to control, however, and subject to frequent abuses. There has been a proliferation of door-to-door and on-the-street collections in recent years, and it has become difficult to walk a single block in any direction in some cities without getting a collection can shaken under one's nose. Many organizations are losing money because of their volunteers' lack of tact and courtesy. In addition, there are just so many times anyone is going to dig into his or her pocket in a single day to drop something into the pot. Our citizenry also is becoming wary of sidewalk collectors who invent charities on the spot to relieve the public of its money. Better organized charities have recognized these problems, and reinforce their volunteer fund drives with an effective program of national publicity that identifies the charity, its cause, the dates for its appeal, and the uses for funds collected.

The next level of volunteer involvement is represented by organizations which use volunteers in implementing programs, but in which the volunteer still has no participation in management. It is at this level that the training and management of volunteers is of greater concern, because in many instances the volunteer is the organization in the public eye. More important, the effectiveness of an organization's program is directly affected by the volunteer's performance. Scouting is a good example of volunteer involvement at this level. The Scout Master is an extension of the scouting program, and he has specific program responsibilities which require specialized skills. He is entrusted not only with the implementation of the scouting program, but also with the well-being of the youngsters participating in it. He requires training and management to ensure that he performs his role effectively. He also does a job that the organization itself could not do with paid staff. There are simply too many cities, communities, and neighborhoods, too many interested boys, and too little money to be able to carry on such a program with salaried employees. But as important as he is, the volunteer at this level still does not play a role in managing the organization, nor in determining its goals and policies.

It is possible for a well-organized, socially useful, and highly-motivated organization to become dominated almost totally by its volunteers. Many organizations are volunteer-oriented to such a high degree that unsalaried personnel have gradually played increasingly important roles in their management. Sometimes volunteers are qualified and trained to perform management roles, but more often they are not. Volunteer participation can become oppressive to an organization's paid staff, and damaging to its programs.

Take for example the organization which for our purposes here we will call the American Association for the Doing of Good Deeds. The association is one of the nation's oldest and most revered nonprofit institutions. Its volunteers are always there in times of war and natural disaster, and its programs in health, welfare, youth affairs, and public and personel safety are well known to most Americons, and emulated by many other organizations. The association prides itself on being run almost totally by volunteers, and its thousands of chapters throughout the country are, for the most part, staffed and managed by unsalaried personnel. That the association performs a vital and praise-worthy function in our society is above question. But its heavy reliance on volunteer staff has had a peculiar side effect on its management at the national level. The national organization has become the tool of its volunteers, and decisions frequently are made—or not made—on the basis of second-guessing how its vast army of volunteers might react.

As a result, the organization has remained basically static in an era when the nonprofit community as a whole is struggling to meet the challenge of social change. The association agonized for months over the decision whether to initiate a drug abuse program, and eventually settled on joining an innocuous and ineffective national "public information" council. Even though many of its young volunteers were, of their own accord, opening highly successful store-front drug counselling programs, the organization rejected incorporating these into its national program on the grounds that its more conservative volunteers would react negatively to "coddling" drug abusers. In another instance, its experience in providing social welfare services to individuals and families in one sector of the society offered a sound basis from which it could have expanded to meet the emerging needs of urban racial minorities. It chose not to do so, purportedly on the grounds that its charter—granted in the late 19th Century—had no provision for undertaking such programs, but in reality because it feared the reaction of its largely white, middle-class volunteers to the move.

Perhaps the greatest perversion of its purpose by volunteer domination occurred during the war in Southeast Asia. The association throughout its history has made much of its international and politically neutral character. The passions of the Viet Nam war, however, saw that neutrality fly out the window, propelled by the heavy boot of jingoism among its volunteers. Pushed by its volunteer policy-makers, the national organization abandoned common sense—and many would say human decency—to become an advocate of the U.S. government's position on one of the major issues of dispute in negotiations to end the conflict. With flags waving in the breeze of their own rhetoric, its volunteers cheered the association on as it adopted the federal administration's line with increasing vehemence. Dissenters from this policy within the organization were accused of various forms of treason from the mild—"peacenik" —to the virulent—"aiding and abetting the enemy."

Meanwhile, the paid administrators of the association sat in Washington and wondered why public donations to the organization were declining. They puzzled over a decreasing interest in its programs among young people, and a rising hostility among blacks and other minorities. They justified stagnation in the association's programs on the grounds that its volunteers wanted things to remain the same, even as the nation and the world were changing. The organization had become the victim of its volunteers who, recognizing that they were beyond the control of the association, lost sight of its broader social goals and used it as an instrument to perpetuate their own prejudices. The level of greatest volunteer involvement is, of course, the board of directors. Here volunteer influence over all aspects of an organization's management is most keenly felt, and the responsibility of volunteers to the institution they serve is greatest. We have already discussed at some length the responsibilities and structure of the board of directors, and there is no need to repeat that discussion here. The important thing to remember about the board is that it is made up of volunteers, and they are as much in need of management as volunteer personnel at any other level.

Just as is the case with paid staff, volunteers must have clearly defined tasks that further the goals of the organization or institution. Volunteer personnel need organization and training, and while they may be honestly motivated to do good, their interest essentially lies elsewhere. The wise nonprofit manager ensures that their work meets real needs of the organization, and that they are held accountable for their performance. Otherwise, managers may well find themselves expending considerable staff time and effort to do correctly what a volunteer, though well-intentioned, botched. And volunteers, even at the board level, must never be permitted to divert an organization from its goals and the programs or services it provides. Our nonprofit community plays too important a role in society to allow it to be perverted as a tool of the worst of the profit motives, rather than nurtured as a healthy counterbalance to the attitudes and functions of the profit sector.

People and Procedure

Procedure must be one of the most abused words of the English language. It is used as an excuse for irrational behavior, puffed up to Olympian proportions, worshipped as that which giveth and taketh away in the day-to-day existence of an organization. Procedure also is ignored, allowed to grow weed-like through the cracks and crevices in an institution's structure, cursed as the reason why nothing ever gets done. Poor procedure. It deserves much more respect and careful attention, especially among nonprofit organizations where it can mean anything from policy on sick leave to implementation of goals.

In reality, procedure is nothing more—or less—than the way things get accomplished. Procedure is a tool, a mechanism which enables an organization to perform those functions it establishes for itself, determine how effectively they are being performed, and at what cost. There is no fixed Law of the Universe called Procedure from which all human activity flows and to which it is answerable. Rather, there are a multitude of approaches open to organizations and institutions in the successful pursuit of their goals and the sound management of themselves toward that end. Because procedure is a function of structure, like structure it is a changing and growing thing, an element of the life itself of an organization. But procedure that is applicable to one organization may have no value whatsoever to another. One institution's procedure is another's chaos.

It is not uncommon that an an organization, caught up in economic pressures and the vastness of human need, creates a structure and programs without considering the procedure necessary to make them work. The opposite side of the same coin is the organization which is weak in both structure and program, and creates a highly elaborate procedure to disguise its internal ineffectiveness. Most organizations, however, fall somewhere between these extremes; they possess a degree of structure, they have developed programs which are more or less worthwhile and effective, and they have some kind of procedure for their internal management and external performance. They manage to survive for years, attempting vast projects with half-vast management, because somehow the money was always there for them to carry on. If these organizations and institutions were poorly managed and fundamentally inefficient, these shortcomings were written off as just the nature of the nonprofit beast. But the time has come when the attitudes of the public about the performance of nonprofits are changing, while at the same time, more and more is being demanded of the nonprofit community. Nonprofits no longer can ignore sound management principles, and one of the most basic of these is procedure.

Procedure is a process of three parts—action, reaction, and adaptation. "Action" is those activities which must be engaged in to perform the function already established as worthy by an organization. "Reaction" is the means of determining whether action is producing desired results in the most efficient manner possible. "Adaptation" is a determination to take whatever steps necessary to make an organization or institution more effective and efficient. Procedure, in other words, is the direction or redirection of energies and resources in the service of a predetermined end.

Or, to attack this concept at a different level, turning the screwdriver in the right direction with the right amount of force is the procedure that gets your screw out of the wall.

Second, procedure is related directly to goal setting. Because goals must be defined in a way which suggests their implementation, they also suggest the procedure for that implementation. Knowing what steps are necessary to accomplish a goal is not the same thing as performing them. But by defining the steps, an organization begins to define the procedure for accomplishing them. To carry an earlier example one step further, if we define our goal as preservation of the environment by legal action against those who pollute it, we have established several steps for its implementation—identifying polluters, gathering evidence, preparing for trial, and so forth. If the steps actually are to be performed, *procedure* must be established for determining what constitutes pollution, how those who are responsible are identified, who prepares and argues the case, what happens after the court renders a decision, etc. In other words, a series of specific actions are spelled out in *procedure,* which makes implementation and achievement possible. This is an example of the "action" element of procedure.

If an organization with this goal is to function efficiently, however, it must have some means of ensuring that these actions are being performed, and being performed with the desired results. There must be a system for keeping track of the number of polluters identified, the progress of cases already in the works, the outcome of civil suits, and the cost of this activity to the organization. The organization requires documented records of its work and its impact, as well as a means for reporting this information within its own structure and to the public at large. Such records-keeping and reporting, however, are more than mere statistical exercises. This process should also be conclusory, showing clearly that an organization is or is not doing its job, where its strengths and weaknesses lie, how much time and money is being spent in pursuit of its goals, and what steps can or must be taken to improve efficiency and effectiveness. Otherwise the organization literally does not know what it is doing. This is procedure as "reaction."

The options open to an organization or institution in developing reactive procedure are many. Organizations may survey the recipients of their services, for example, to determine how well they are achieving their goals through the eyes of those for whom the programs were designed. They may establish files on the frequency, location, number, and use of projects, and require that such information be reported to management on a regular basis. Institutions may require that employees and volunteers keep time sheets recording the hours spent in pursuit of any given task. However the record-keeping system is set up, it must have some safeguards built into it to ensure that the information reported has some relation to reality. The Overbite Fund, for example, is fond of reporting that it "provided technical assistance to more than 58,000 professionals in the last fiscal year." This means, in reality, it mailed 58,000 pamphlets. The Fund also reports that its field service offices "participated in 20,000 cooperative public service projects," which translates as someone was there to answer the telephone when it rang. In this instance, the records kept are meaningless because they do not show the true nature of the tasks performed. Whatever procedure is employed, it must be used so that the organization can discover the truth about itself, and not hide its inadequacies in that strangest of all languages, bureaucratese.

One of the most important facets of reactive procedure is accounting and financial management. For a full discussion of nonprofit accounting and its importance to an organization, see Paul Bennett's highly-readable *Up Your Accountability*, published by Taft Products, Inc., in its "Non-Profit-Ability" series. Financial management is a subject worthy of much more detailed treatment than it will be afforded here in this effort to look at the overall management of the nonprofit community. There are two major points to be made here: nonprofits should—and must—be held accountable for the public funds entrusted to their stewardship, and the procedure employed in accounting for those funds must be no less stringent than that of the profit sector.

No profit-making organization would last long in the marketplace if it was as casual toward and ignorant of proper accounting procedure as many nonprofits. There are major differences in the rules and techniques of nonprofit accounting which set it apart from accounting for profit. Profit-motivated corporations expend revenue in the pursuit of income which benefits their owners. Nonprofit organizations spend their money in the performance of services and programs which benefit the society in general. As Bennett points out, "We may say that income is the measure of a nonprofit's capability. Expenses are a measure of its fulfillment of its purpose. While a profit enterprise incurs expenses in order to generate income, a nonprofit acquires income in order to make expenditures." This distinction is quite correct in terms of how the nonprofit organization keeps its books, and treats its financial statements. But it also is true that the nonprofit which manages its resources wisely performs its function more effectively, and its success in fulfilling its purpose generates more income by attracting greater public support. In the final analysis, the motivation for the sound fiscal management of the nonprofit is not so very different from that of the profit enterprise.

Demands that nonprofits exercise greater financial responsibility in the management of their affairs are steadily increasing. As of this writing, the nonprofit community is coming under scrutiny in the United States Senate, and no one can say what the outcome of these hearings may be. But revelations in those hearings have cast doubt on the integrity and value of much of the entire nonprofit sector. Some organizations have been discovered to be spending such huge sums on administration that very little of the public's money actually gets used to benefit those for whom it was donated. One of the nation's most respected institutions for orphaned boys—which everyone will remember was kept going in the 1930s against enormous odds by Spencer Tracy and Mickey Rooney—was discovered to have generated a multi-million dollar profit over the years, and is now giving money away to other institutions making its administrators appear to be either rogues or fools or both.

In addition, new tax laws make it imperative for nonprofits to be able to account accurately for how their money is acquired and spent. Poor financial management could result in the loss of nonprofit status for tax purposes. Finally, the mentality that once made it honorable for nonprofits to run a substantial deficit each year increasingly is being challenged by institutional donors. Major foundations and corporations are less and less willing to finance a nonprofit's deficit, and the persistence among many institutions that someone will turn up with the cash to balance the books at the end of the year is becoming a highly dangerous form of self-deception. The rules of the game are changing, and nonprofit managers who do not recognize this fact, and respond accordingly, may soon find themselves looking for a new line of work.

Nonprofits always are torn in opposing directions when it comes to the management of money. On the one hand, there is a certain elation to spending large sums to perform good deeds that makes it very easy to overlook such mundane considerations as accurate bookkeeping and questions of cost-effectiveness. Many nonprofits feel—and rightly so—that there are some programs which must be undertaken regardless of their cost, and that in such cases the necessity of meeting human needs outweighs balanced books. On the other hand, nonprofits are keenly aware of how difficult it is to raise money, and as a general rule, they want to make every dollar count in the attainment of their goals. Such fiscal schizophrenia is widespread in the nonprofit sector, and we see its symptoms in alternating fits of heavy-handed, tough-minded control over the purse strings and orgies of spending abandon. Nonprofits must recognize, however, that it is important to their fiscal health to know how much is being spent where and for what purpose, efficiently or not. Wherever possible they must incorporate an accounting procedure that enables them at the least to know at any given moment where the public's money is going, and at best, that it is being spent effectively to further their goals.

But it is difficult for any organization or institution to measure its effectiveness because of the intangibility of its products. Only rarely is a nonprofit engaged in an activity which produces some measurable end, and most often an institution's work is aimed at producing a social benefit such as "promoting international understanding," or "fostering cultural betterment." Given the competitiveness of the nonprofit marketplace, however, it is becoming more and more imperative that nonprofits develop some means of quantifying the effectiveness of their programs, no matter how intangible they may be.

The nonprofit organization can borrow successfully from its profit-motivated neighbors in this area. The techniques of market research which have proven successful in determining who buys how much soap and why can be adapted to measuring utilization and effectiveness of nonprofit programs. Robert Jordan Dubin, an experienced marketing executive in both the profit and nonprofit sectors, directed a highly interesting and informative study of two nonprofit programs for major institutional donors. As reported in an article in *Management Review Magazine* in January 1973, the study adapted commercial market research techniques to the measurement of two similar cultural programs.* Dubin points out that the study sought to determine whether the programs (1) were successful, (2) were accomplishing their objectives, (3) deserved continued support at the same or different levels, and (4) how they might be improved.

His findings and methodology deserve greater exposure than can be given them here. But his conclusions are significant enough in their implications for nonprofits that they should be quoted at length:

". . . Commercial marketing methods can be adapted to nonprofit programs whose results heretofore have defied quantitative measurement. Moreover, these methods result in 'hard' data on the effectiveness of such programs and enable donor and recipient institutions to make more precise decisions about what programs to fund and how to spend that money once it is given . . .

". . . This study indicates that commercial marketing strategies can be applied to programs at the proposal stage, before funds have been granted. Nonprofit money managers can determine in advance which programs are worthy of funding and which will result in the greatest benefit to the individuals, many of them desperately in need, to whom they are directed . . .

"We view this research as a pragmatic review of organizational effectiveness and program success, rather than as an academic exercise in human behavioral response. The research design focused on those aspects of each program that are most important, in terms of the program's aims, and was tailored to develop reliable, scientifically valid data in sufficient depth and detail to aid decision makers in their choices . . .

---

*Dubin, Robert Jordan, "Determining Results in the Generosity Business," *Management Review Magazine*, January 1973; published by the American Management Association, 135 West 50th Street, New York, N.Y. 10020.

". . . We were not seeking to determine success in terms of the degree of acceptance of the program, or, in other words, whether more individuals liked it than did not. Rather, the research goal was addressed to a specific management problem: Is the funding agency spending its money wisely?"

Which brings us in good time to procedure as adaptation. Adaptive procedure is at the heart of the decision-making process in the management of nonprofit organizations and institutions. When active and reactive procedures are working at their optimum, adaptation is simply a matter of making choices, of applying resources to those programs and services which are most effective and withholding them from those which aren't. Procedure at this level enables the nonprofit manager to see new needs as they emerge and move to meet them if the performance of his organization indicates it is capable of contributing to their solution. Procedure in management is the sum of procedure at the action and reaction levels. All that an organization is, all that it can become, all that it is capable of being unfolds here in the decisions that a manager makes, based on the information and record of performance his organization generates.

But it also is here that the flow of energies procedure is created to channel begins to move in the opposite direction. Once the decision is made, it must be implemented, and adaptation provides for the fact of the decision, its implications, the new or different work it requires to filter back down through the organization to the action level. Thus we see that procedure is a progressive cycle which moves an organization from point to point in its development toward attainment of its goals. Procedure, contrary to the ugly connotations of rigidity and stagnation that it has come to have, is a growing thing.

Which, in turn, brings us to the third important concept of procedure which nonprofits must keep constantly in mind. As the subtitle of this section suggests, procedure is intertwined with people. The nonprofit staff must share in shaping an organization's procedures, must be made to understand why they are necessary and why they work. Procedure is a tool of management to direct or redirect the labors of those who do the work of the organization. But procedure cannot ignore the needs and the attitudes, the human-ness of the people who follow it. When procedure ceases to be rational or humane, it ceases to be effective. In the end, it becomes self-destructive and can prevent an organization from doing the job it has set out for itself. The nonprofit organization and its staff have enough problems performing their jobs without the added burden of worshipping at the feet of procedure.

People and procedure working in concert, within the context of a clearly-defined set of goals and a strong structure, are the most important resources the nonprofit community has.

But what is it, exactly, that they do?

4 NONPROFIT PROGRAMS... OR, WHY DOESN'T SOMEBODY DO SOMETHING?

"... now I want to make this clear. We have a program for that, too. They have no monopoly on concern in this area ... you've heard tonight that we don't care about these questions or problems or issues or what-have-you. Well, let me tell you that we are no less concerned than they are. We have programs, too. And they are good programs, and they are our programs. We have programs. . . ."

> —from a statement by an unsuccessful presidential candidate during a televised political debate, circa 1960

It's time for a tough question. It's one which no one likes to hear in the nonprofit community, but it is one which should be asked, and asked more often. The question is this: How effectively is the nonprofit sector functioning in our society? Or, put a different way: Of the estimated 1.5 million nonprofit organizations in the United States today, which offer programs and services of real benefit to our society, and which would we not miss if they closed their doors tomorrow?

Anybody care to tackle that one? The answer of many nonprofit executives likely would be "Everybody else's but mine." That's an understandable response, but brings us no closer to resolving the issue. The cynic would point out that for all of the $25 billion and some loose change spent last year in support of nonprofits, we still are plagued by injustice, madness, disease, poverty, inequality, greed, hunger, illiteracy, misunderstanding, not enough of a lot of things and too much of others and nothing works the way it's supposed to any more. One has to admit that is a difficult argument to refute.

Still the issue remains, are our nonprofits doing the job they're supposed to, or aren't they? There is seldom any confusion about how well the profit sector is doing. We have created an elaborate system of economic indicators which tell us when we're up and when we're down. But there are no commonly accepted indicators of societal health against which the effectiveness of the nonprofit community as a whole may be measured. The only measurement available to us in real numbers is the amount of money spent in the nonprofit sector, and a nose count of the organizations and institutions in existence today. There is no way for the society as a whole to determine the results of that spending or of the programs of these organizations and institutions.

Part of our problems in answering this question arises from the definition of the word nonprofit. The dictionary definition—"not entered into to yield a profit . . . as in a nonprofit association"—shows just how little we understand the word and the concepts behind it. We realize that there are many different kinds of nonprofit entities—special interest groups, professional associations, social service organizations, fraternal groups, labor unions, colleges and universities. We recognize that these widely divergent groups often hold conflicting points of view, ideals, and aims. Yet in most instances we treat them as if they are all of the same cloth, we often expect them to demonstrate the same degree of selflessness in their goals, and we imbue them all, mistakenly, with more or less the same noble motivation. Such blurring of distinctions among nonprofits contributes substantially to our inability to determine which are useful to our society as a whole, and worthy of our continued support.

But even granting such diversity in the nonprofit population, the fact that there is no ready answer to the question we have posed here says a great deal about the kinds of programs and services engaged in by nonprofits. It seems obvious that if the nonprofit sector were functioning properly, the question would answer itself; we would see the results clearly in specific improvements in the quality of life in our society. But the truth of the matter is that far too often nonprofits themselves do not know what they are doing, nor why they are doing it. And because of poor management, many nonprofits have good reason not to want the results of their activities widely known.

If a nonprofit is to survive, prosper, and grow, it must ensure that its programs are managed efficiently and produce their intended results. All that we have discussed to this point, all of our concern for effective organization, structure, goal setting, personnel, and procedure comes into its sharpest focus in the issue of program. When an institution is well structured and effectively managed, its energies and resources are directed toward developing, implementing, refining, and administering its program. When it is not, an organization will spend its time and money in a fruitless search for something to do, a kind of programmatic blind man's buff. It eventually will begin to believe, or delude itself into believing, that such unorganized, unintelligent, and unmanaged activity is "program." An organization also must understand thoroughly what it can do and what it can't. It must be willing to admit that there are some problems which are beyond its capabilities to solve. It must be willing to look to others for help when needed, and it must know when to give up and quit wasting resources that could be better spent.

The latter is a very important point, and one which nonprofits are loath to face. No one wants to admit defeat or that he has outlived his usefulness, and certainly no one wants to be out of a job. Yet there are clearly instances when a nonprofit has either served its purpose and no longer is needed, or is so ineffective that it no longer is doing good. It is neither cynical nor paranoid to ask ourselves what would some of our larger health organizations do if a cure were found for cancer, birth defects, respiratory diseases? Where would our multi-million dollar protectors of the environment redirect their energies if our society awoke one morning and decided the time had come to exercise self-restraint in the exploitation of our natural resources? By the same token, what if many of our small- and medium-sized organizations and institutions were to recognize that they no longer perform a useful function, or are needlessly duplicating the functions of others? Would they seek new directions, new challenges, or would they stubbornly cling to their own small piece of nonprofit turf, regardless of what their senses told them of their value?

The answers to all these questions lie in how nonprofits perceive program in relation to their own purposes, and to the larger role of the nonprofit community as a whole. To develop and manage programs effectively, nonprofits first must understand what programs are.

Programs are the manifestation of our society's collective concern about a problem or an issue, the reasons why nonprofit organizations and institutions are created. Nonprofits must understand programs as the actualization of their goals, that is, ideals in the process of becoming realities, and that these ideals existed as abstractions in our social consciousness long before the nonprofit was created. The nonprofit, in this sense, is the actor on the stage of our struggle for social betterment, speaking the lines and making the motions that we ourselves have created for it. Programs are actions for social good which keep the ever-present tension between profit and nonprofit motives in balance, imperfect though it may be. Programs do not exist because there are nonprofits, but rather nonprofits are the mechanism society has chosen to carry out programs.

Without meaningful and effective programs, nonprofits have no rationale for existence, and certainly no right to demands on our money or our concern. The organization which does not structure and manage itself to perform its programs effectively is not only useless—but it also is guilty of moral fraud. Such an organization, by its existence and avowed aims, is entering into a contract with the public which it cannot perform, and falsely raising the hopes of those who need and believe in its services. Our society, consciously or not, looks to the nonprofit community to fulfill a role we cannot or will not perform otherwise. The organization which accepts for itself the responsibility to participate in that role, and fails to do so, is wasting time and resources which could be redirected to socially useful functions. There is enough waste, more than enough unfulfilled promises in our society. That is one of the reasons why there are nonprofit institutions.

Program begins as a concept of how to further or promote some social gain which already has been determined an area of concern in the goals of a nonprofit organization. This is a critical point in the development of sound programs, because it is here that an organization defines the problem to be solved, and, in so doing, defines the plan of action the organization believes will be effective. Nonprofits must be sure they inform themselves fully of all the facets and repercussions of a problem before undertaking any action to correct it. No matter how pressing the need may seem, nor how great the desire to do good, an organization must not take a single step until it has adequately defined the issue it confronts. It must gather accurate data on the extent of the problem, the kinds and number of people affected by it, the options open to it in approaching a solution, and the potential cost of those options.

Many nonprofits make the error of equating their perception of a problem with its definition. They create programs based on what they think they see, rather than on an accurate assessment of reality. For example, an organization concerned about low-cost housing for the poor may convince itself easily that there is inadequate housing for the poor because there are not enough physical structures to house them. It determines that it will launch a program to build more housing for low-income families. It will not be long before that organization comes to realize that it lacks the resources to undertake a building program large enough in scope to be meaningful. It will begin to look for alternatives to construction, and most likely—based on the performance pattern of many nonprofits—settle on an advocate role; if the organization cannot build housing, it will convince others to. It will create guidelines for construction of housing for the poor, "educate" the government at various levels of the need for adequate housing for the poor, and "inform" the general public of this need. Now this activity will consume an enormous amount of time and resources, generate tons of paper and millions of words, even make headlines for and attract funding to the organization. But it will not result in more adequate housing for the poor.

And the reason is quite simple. Adequate housing for the poor is more than a question of buildings. It is an issue involving prejudices, zoning regulations, construction costs, the housing market, the perceptions of others of the needs of the poor in relation to the poor's perceptions of themselves. Low-income housing is a highly complex issue which cuts across a wide range of problems throughout our society, and no amount of guidelines, educating, and informing will be sufficient to touch all those problems and offer sensible solutions. And it must be recognized that we already know there is a shortage of adequate housing for low-income families, and that as a society we possess the resources to do something about it. We have, for whatever reasons, chosen not to redirect our resources to this issue. But because our nonprofit in this case sees, or chooses to see, only one aspect of the problem, it will go on for years writing guidelines, testifying before congressional committees, and issuing reports. Eventually it will grow weaker and less effective, go out of existence, or simply close its eyes to the fact that it is ineffective, and press on.

In this instance, a nonprofit saw what was in reality a series of interrelated problems as but a single issue. The organization would have fared better had it originally defined its goal differently, and created a number of programs to attack as many facets of the problem as it had determined it was capable of performing effectively. Had this organization fully informed itself of the nature and the scope of the problem in the beginning, it might have been able to effect a program for change. Instead, it acted on rhetoric alone, and wound up expending its resources uselessly. Equally important, the nonprofit was so poorly managed that it could not, or would not, recognize that its program was ineffective, and it failed to take steps to change the program to make it more responsive to the problem.

If our mythical nonprofit were not so caught up in its own needs and wants, it might see other solutions to low-cost housing needs. For example, it should have realized that housing is an issue which very much affects the profit sector of our society, and it should have co-opted that sector into its program. Few builders are going to construct low-cost housing unless it is profitable for them to do so. No one is going to live in low-cost housing by choice, not even the poor, unless there are adequate shopping and personal services available nearby. A little more thought and a little less rhetoric by our nonprofit would have brought the realization that some of the options open to it in dealing with the low-cost housing issue include research into adaptation of inexpensive or pre-fabricated housing to multi-unit, low-cost dwellings, using public and private funds to encourage business expansion, starting minority-owned businesses and services near or on the site of the housing, and providing services such as job placement for adults and daycare for the children of working mothers. All of these activities, directly or indirectly, would have generated income and attracted the support of the profit sector, while at the same time begun to solve the lack of adequate housing.

But such an approach would have demanded time, thought, planning, and a great deal of hard work. Our nonprofit wanted the problem solved immediately. It didn't want to hear about economic studies and business expansion and all the other tools of the profit-motivated corporate world. It did not want to establish goals, structure, and procedures which would make it possible to begin to solve the problem on a limited scale. Its impatience and lack of careful thought crippled it.

In contrast, let us look for a moment at the National Association for Special Children. It was founded about 50 years ago to provide greater educational, occupational, and social opportunities for handicapped and gifted children. Working with a membership largely of professionals in education and related fields, the association's original goals were to serve the interests of these professionals, to promote equal treatment for handicapped and gifted children in public school systems, and to press for government programs at the national, state, and local levels to meet their special needs. Over the years this legislative function consumed more and more of the association's efforts, and in the 1960s it was recognized as a not-for-profit but taxable organization. In the course of its work, as reporting procedures nationally improved, in part because of the NASC's efforts, the association discovered that there are more than six million physically or mentally handicapped children in the United States, another two million who are exceptionally gifted, and about one million such children who could not be accounted for in the public institutions of our society. In other words, somewhere along the line we had lost one million of our own.

The association recognized through its professional membership that public education and vocational training programs for these children were inadequate. It saw that substantial sums of private money had to be infused into the system if the association was to attain its goals and the needs of these children were to be met. But at the same time, NASC realized that it could not attract this money because it had given up its nonprofit tax status. After careful study and a clear definition of goals, NASC determined what was needed was a new organization that could draw on the experience, expertise, and resources of the association, yet could also attract tax-deductible contributions from the general public and institutional donors. The Foundation for Special Children was born. With the help of professional counsel, the association launched a highly successful campaign to attract support from among its own membership. Today, the foundation is still in its formulative stages, and already is attracting support from other institutional sources. A great deal of time and effort is being expanded to ensure that the foundation will be structured and managed to meet its goals of providing services and programs to benefit directly handicapped and gifted children.

The association is an example of many of the best principles of nonprofit management. It has strong board and administrative leadership, a sound and well-managed structure, clear-cut goals, and the procedure that enabled it to see when a new approach to an old problem was needed. It recognized the need for thorough planning and organization in establishing new programs, and it was willing to do the work necessary to implement them. There is no doubt that the new foundation will thrive and prosper, and perform a useful service for a long-neglected segment of our society. The association is engaged in real and meaningful programs; the advocate of low-cost housing is not.

It would appear that one of the most difficult management tasks for nonprofits to accomplish is to make certain that their programs bear some realistic relationship to their goals. The National Association for the Treatment and Prevention of Malocclusion—our old friend the Overbite Fund—is spending time and effort in the pursuit of programs symptomatic of an organizational drift which carries it farther and farther from its goals. Research into the relationship between malocclusion and the environment is not only silly, but also fundamentally unrelated to what the organization set out to do—help people straighten out their teeth. In addition, its nightmarish structure is not susceptible to establishing procedures for its effective management, rendering it virtually incapable of seeing itself and its operations clearly, and making whatever adjustments are necessary to get functioning properly again—or in this case, for the first time. Not only was the Fund guilty of defining its goals poorly in the first place, but it also was unable to translate those goals into programs of any real benefit. What happens to an organization or institution between the process of setting goals—for better or for worse—and the implementation of those goals that can carry it so far from its original purpose?

Generally, the answer can be found in two highly important factors: management and money. As we have noted before, goals must be defined in a way which suggest the structure for their implementation, which in turn helps to define the procedure—and the kind and number of people—necessary for their attainment. Program is the visible, externally directed manifestation of this process, the actual redirection of the society's resources for social good. Where there is weakness in any link in this chain, program will be weakened to the same degree, and, in fact, so will the total organization. It is true that goals change over the years, that boards, executive directors, and staffs at any given time may be more or less talented and still the organization will survive. But unless procedure properly is developed and adhered to, the organization's programs will never be truly effective. Procedure provides a check on programs, a means of determining their effectiveness in terms of the cost required to produce intended results. The poorly managed nonprofit which not only improperly establishes procedure but also fails to use it has no way of knowing at any given point what it is doing, nor whether its effort is producing the desired results, or any results at all.

Such feedback is essential to the effective management of nonprofits. As is the case with a profit-making corporation, nonprofits must be able to determine that the return on their products justifies the expenditure of their resources. In the nonprofit community, return is real social benefit and the product is program. But the result of mismanagement at this point is the same for both profit and nonprofit organizations—if they spend too much of their resources on an inadequate product they will go out of business.

Money is the second major factor which can mislead an organization away from its purpose. Nonprofits are continually in competition with one another for funds in a limited marketplace. Essentially there are only three sources of funds available to nonprofit organizations: individuals, institutional donors (foundations, the government, other organizations), and business. As a society, we are daily identifying new problems and creating new organizations and institutions to deal with them. The sources of funds, if not the amount itself, however, remain relatively constant, and, in fact, because of new tax laws and other economic pressures, at the moment are shrinking. In addition, the priorities and giving patterns of funding sources themselves are subject to change, as new social issues are uncovered and appear more or less immediately in need of solution. A foundation which several years ago was granting funds to health programs, may decide this year that the state of the environment and sources of energy are more important concerns, and will restructure its giving accordingly. Nonprofits find themselves caught up in a scramble to uncover new sources of funds, or to find new ways to approach as yet untapped existing sources.

The demand for money can produce strange behavior in us all, and this is no less true for nonprofit organizations and institutions. Let's listen in on the Overbite Fund's last staff meeting.

Staffer:
"Say, chief, the Magnanimous Foundation told us it's not funding health programs any more . . . into ecology now."

Executive Director:
"Oh-oh . . . there goes 50 grand a year. What'll we do."

Staffer:
"I dunno. That guy Freebish was around here again yesterday looking for a job. You know, the Ph.D. in landscape gardening who used to be with the Peace Corps?"

Executive Director:
"So?"

Staffer:
"Well, that's ecology, isn't it? I mean maybe we could . . ."

Executive Director:

"Stonely, what are you suggesting?"

Staffer:

"Look we've got to do something. Maybe we could set this Freebish up to study how teeth fit into the whole ecological picture. You know, how a person's teeth affect the way he lives in relation to nature . . . or something."

Executive Director:

"You know, Stonely, you've got something there, I think. Maybe we could convince Magnanimous this is right up their alley. Show 'em we're on top of things. Relevant, as they say."

Staffer:

"Chief, I'll get right on it . . . yeah, the effects of malocclusion on the environment . . . Chief, I think you've got another winner. I don't know how you do it."

Executive Director:

"Thinking, Stonely. I'm always thinking."

This kind of "thinking" is becoming more and more prevalent as the nonprofit dollar becomes more and more elusive. It is correct to the extent that it recognizes that program is the nonprofit's most saleable item. But it is disastrous in its assumption that any program which appears to have any bearing on a donor's interest offers hope of attracting funds.

Program is in reality a nonprofit's only product. Additional revenue may come from membership fees, or the sale of publications, but non-profits would have neither members nor anything to publish were it not for program. When a competently managed organization can demonstrate that its program is economically sound, properly administered, and socially useful, it can build a strong case for support in the nonprofit marketplace, and usually will find that support. When management is bungled, and program is vague and without demonstrable results, no amount of dressing up or covering over these shortcomings is going to delude an intelligent donor into giving it financial support. A nonprofit may be able to hide its inefficiencies and poor results for a time, but eventually its failings come back to haunt it in declining public and private support.

Nor is it any easier for an organization to get away with pretending to be something that it is not. The Overbite Fund clearly isn't qualified or organized to make much of a contribution to the solution of our environmental problems. Trying to appear that it is in the long run will cost the organization more in resources than it will gain in funding, and the Fund will find itself caught in a vicious cycle which spins 'round and 'round to the tune of "try anything if it will bring in money." There is a great deal of this kind of dancing and weaving going on in our educational institutions, who scan the horizon in search of an unwary donor, and seek to ambush him with new programs built on the flimsy foundation of educational faddism. Who knows how many college presidents are this moment sitting in how many foundation offices trying to explain that their four-year liberal arts colleges are different from all the other four-year liberal arts colleges because they have a degree program in welding for women, or are teaching Bantu to their elementary education majors. It might be more profitable for those college presidents to be explaining that our public schools turn out about one million functional illiterates each year, and they want to cut out some of the flighty irrelevance and teach kids how to read. Female welders and Bantu-speaking school teachers are a luxury our educational institutions can afford only after they have demonstrated that they are solving some of the more fundamental problems of learning in our society. Until they can, it will be difficult for them to convince donors that other concerns are worthy of priority in their giving patterns.

Well-organized and managed nonprofits are no less affected by the tightening nonprofit market. But they also recognize that to compete successfully for the nonprofit dollar they must perform their function more effectively, find good cause to extend their services and programs to different or emerging segments of our society, or create new programs that provide innovative solutions for existing problems, all within the framework of their capabilities and record of achievement. Because they can measure the effectiveness of their programs, they can identify changes in the needs of the markets they serve much more readily than nonprofits who lack the proper management tools. They are the first to recognize the need for additional programs, or overhauls of existing ones, and therefore the first to bring their cases—well-documented—to donors. Moreover, properly managed nonprofits also are able to recognize sooner when funding sources are reshuffling their priorities, and either alter their programs in a meaningful way to continue to attract money from existing sources, or prepare their case appropriately for presentation to new sources of funds.

Nonprofits must not allow the pressures of immediate financial need to blind them to their purpose. An organization which readily abandons or distorts its goals at the first sniff of new sources of money is dooming itself to failure. For the farther away from its original purpose an organization gets, the more difficult it becomes to manage. Its resources become diverted from the pursuit of its goals to the pursuit of funds, and, assuming it had a valid program to begin with, its program suffers accordingly. Such an organization will find it spends less and less time administering its programs and more time trying to wring additional money out of them. The nonprofit will enter a downward spiral of inefficiency and futility which can lead only to stagnation.

But what happens when social priorities shift, or an organization finds it has managed itself too well, and there is simply no longer the resources or the need to continue its programs? There are many organizations and institutions which have been forced into bankruptcy by changing social attitudes. Yesterday's problems are in many instances the socially acceptable behavior of today, and that, too, will change in the years to come. Nonprofits must accept that they are mortal, and that the time will come when they must face the closing of their doors, whatever the reasons.

In the case of nonprofits which are shut down, in effect, by their own inefficiencies, society has suffered no great loss. We may be grateful that such institutions have finally choked on their own incompetence, and that the drain of these institutions on our nonprofit resources has subsided. We also may be grateful when an organization's life comes to a close because it has accomplished what it set out to do, and did it well. We are all the better for its existence, and its experience, resources, and personnel can be redirected to other organizations or institutions in the nonprofit sector which need them. In either case, the society and the nonprofit community itself are better off.

It is unfortunate, however, that the laws of the profit marketplace do not apply as readily to the nonprofit sector, and that we must often bear an ineffective organization's sickness and final passing over so long a period of time. Because we so often fail to see the realities of nonprofit organization and management, we are willing to suffer all manner of abuses in the nonprofit sector which we would not tolerate in the profit sector. We are willing to let many of our nonprofits pass off paper-shuffling as program, and turn our heads the other way when it comes time to total the results. But we owe it to ourselves to make nonprofits as fully accountable for their actions—or inactions—as we do profit-motivated enterprises. More important, nonprofits owe it to themselves to oversee their activities to ensure effectiveness and efficiency.

It is, after all, their lives which depend on it.

5 PAYING FOR IT... WHERE THE NONPROFIT DOLLAR COMES FROM, AND HOW TO GET IT

In the beginning, we stated that this book is about money. So far we have discussed money in terms of management, or how nonprofit organizations can redirect effectively society's financial resources for society's gain. But to do so, nonprofits must attract and hold on to the nonprofit dollar. They must understand how the nonprofit money market works, who has that money, and how to get it. Money and its complications generally is the part of management which nonprofits dislike the most, but it also is what most often occupies the greatest amount of their time and energies.

Vast numbers of small- and medium-sized nonprofit organizations and institutions in our society live under the oppression of hand-to-mouth funding. Either they do not know where to get money, or how to attract it in substantial sums over relatively long periods of time. Such oppression is usually self-inflicted, resulting from the failure of a nonprofit to recognize its relationship to the profit segment, and its unwillingness to adapt proven profit-oriented management principles to its own operations. Most nonprofits view raising money as a necessary evil which they must force themselves to be a party to in order to carry on their work. They believe, wrongly, that because they are society's conscience they should be above issues of money. Somehow, nonprofits feel, dollars should pour in to support their cause from a public that has a moral obligation to recognize their worth. This attitude produces nothing but the tension of constant frustration in an organization, and, together with poor management practices, constitutes a self-fulfilling prophecy.

This wrong-mindedness sows the seeds of a sickness that is peculiar to nonprofits. Organizations and institutions sometimes develop a kind of universal paranoia toward the profit segment in which they see themselves as victims of a conspiracy among those who have money to deprive them of it. "People" just don't understand how important their work is, how serious the problems are they seek to solve. "Big corporations" control all the money anyway, and they're not going to give up any of it for (insert the cause of your choice) when they can use it to make more money. "Big corporations" and "people" control foundations, and they only grant money to (a) their friends, (b) their friends' friends, or (c) organizations and institutions that don't rock the boat and aren't doing anything important. As for the federal government, who has time to fill out all those forms, and once you do, there's no guarantee that you'll get the money at all, or in time to do any good. Nonprofits so afflicted wind up wallowing about in self-pity, whining that they really don't need money, that they can survive on noble thoughts alone, and no one's going to listen to them, anyway. And they're right. Because they do not try to raise funds properly and use them effectively, no one does listen, and they must operate continually at subsistence level.

It is obvious that in reality there are no "profit" dollars and no "nonprofit" dollars; there are only sums of the same money being spent to attain different ends. The money available to the nonprofit community all comes from the same basic source: profit-motivated enterprises, be they individual or corporate. Money is channeled to nonprofit enterprises through taxation, voluntary contribution, or direct solicitation. No matter how a nonprofit receives support, it is axiomatic that the only way an organization gets it is to seek it out, as vulgar as that may seem to many.

Money is an absolutely essential fact of life for any organization. So much so, in fact, that decisions about raising it—how much, from whom, and for what purpose—are the most significant choices a nonprofit can make. Raising money is a highly focused process with a single clear-cut goal. It takes a great deal of experienced and creative thinking to devise a successful development program, and the process is kept going by three key elements—careful planning, the right people, and the proper tools. Experience teaches that a sound development program meets five criteria:

▶ it is comprehensive, taking into account the needs of the total organization over a specific period of planned growth;

▶ it is cohesive, eliciting and involving the efforts of all elements of an organization or institution in a single overall goal;

▶ it is consistent, working toward its goal through the implementation of a fully crafted strategy for approaching the nonprofit marketplace;

▶ it is creative, utilizing innovative methods to identify donors, motivate them to recognize the value of an organization's programs, and convince them to restructure their giving priorities accordingly; and, finally,

▶ a successful program is guided by the best principles of marketing and communications which have been proven valid in the commercial marketplace.

It takes little intelligent observation to understand that to raise money effectively an organization must first know how much money it needs and for what purposes. But to know that, a nonprofit must first be able to identify where it is spending money now. It must document costs incurred in establishing and running programs, keeping its house, paying its debts, constructing its buildings, paying its employees, printing its literature, and raising its money. The properly managed nonprofit has established procedure for monitoring these costs accurately, and can, at any given point, determine with relative ease where it stands financially. Equally important, it also can project what it will cost to expand its programs, staff, or physical facilities over a given period of its growth. It should be emphasized that current costs and future projections must be related to real expenditures and real needs. An organization cannot *think* that it needs $2 million to meet its commitments over the next five years; it must *know* how and where it will expand to continue to serve its goals, and as much as is humanly possible, precisely how much such expansion will cost.

One of the most common stories of the nonprofit sector is the tale of the escalating expenditures. Time and again, organizations with sloppy accounting procedure estimate the cost of a given project, only to find that it costs twice as much. This most frequently occurs because nonprofits simply do not know at any moment where their money is being spent and what it is being spent for. The annual budget says the organization is spending $150,000 in salaries, when a new pay raise went into effect only a month ago, and the organization actually is spending $165,000. The development "plan" says a new building will cost $5.5 million to build, while construction costs, uncontrolled by any monitoring procedure, are rising at the rate of $10,000 a month. There is no end to examples of this kind, all of which point to poor management of financial resources which makes it impossible for organizations to determine how much money they are spending for what purpose, and how much they will have to spend in the future.

It also should be emphasized that every program or activity which requires money to function, whether or not it produces income, must be accounted for in an organization's financial planning. Often in discussing potential development programs, nonprofits will say, "Oh, don't worry about the membership program; it pays for itself." But the membership program does not exist in isolation from all other operations of the organization, and its function is not to pay for itself but to generate income to support the organization as a whole. No program is "paying for itself" if an organization has to borrow or scrounge funds to meet its payroll because it is engaged in other programs and services which are "not paying for themselves." This is called not being able to see the forest for the trees. No organization is only a collection or bits and pieces of program and management. It also is a whole entity which must be kept sight of and whose functions must be understood if a financial development program is to have any value. Otherwise, in the long run, an organization is only stealing money from itself to pay for scattered, isolated programs, when its concern should be directed toward its strength and growth as a whole. If any part of a nonprofit suffers financially, the total organization suffers to the same degree. Likewise, when the total organization is financially healthy, all its parts should benefit. In this sense, *everything* an organization does is directly related to development.

Because this is true, everyone within an organization or institution also is a part of the development process. Bitter and wasteful internal struggles result when nonprofits fail to recognize how and why this is true, and do not properly instruct their staffs in the role they play in raising money. The antiprofit mentality not only produces a disdain for financial concerns among nonprofits, but also creates employees who believe they are not and should not be involved in raising funds. Thus, when the manager of one program sees that a colleague, of his own volition or because of scattered funding policies, is getting more money to run his program when he is not, he feels resentful, and, worse, self-righteous in isolating himself from money questions. It is his responsibility to do good works, he believes, and someone else must make the effort to pay for the luxury of his nobility. Or, if he is more aggressive, he may develop an every-man-for-himself attitude, and engage in internal and external maneuvering to raise funds for his own program, apart from the needs of the organization as a whole. It also is common that an organization will set a development goal, its board will approve it, its executive director will carry the word to the director of development, and everyone will sit back on their hands, and wait for the money to roll in. When it doesn't, the organization fires the development director and hires a new one, or seeks the help of professional fund-raising counsel, or both. That, too, will fail, because all the salaried and volunteer personnel of the organization are looking to everyone but themselves to raise money, when it is clearly their responsibility to do it, for it is they who benefit from it.

The board member, the research scientist, the field worker all are involved in raising money for the organization they serve. In doing so, they are enabling that organization better to meet its goals, which they believe in and truly wish to see fulfilled, or they have no business being there in the first place. The board member must recognize his leadership role, both as a contributor and as a solicitor of funds from among his peers. The scientist must recognize that his research is the basis for attracting funds—a product—and that he has a responsibility to make, or help to make, others understand what he is doing and why to secure funds so that he can go on working. The field worker also has a responsibility to recognize new needs as they are emerging and to help formulate programs to meet them. Programs, like the work of the scientist, are the nonprofit's rationale for existing and for getting money. Everyone who labors in the nonprofit marketplace for whatever cause is directly involved in raising funds for the organization of which he is a part. And there are no exceptions.

It also is important that nonprofits individually understand the nature of their relationship to the nonprofit marketplace as a whole. Each organization or institution should become aware of its position in that marketplace in terms of the programs and services which are unique to it. Or, stated another way, each nonprofit must try to identify what it is about itself that distinguishes it from all competing organizations. It also is necessary for nonprofits to know how they are perceived by potential donors within the marketplace before they enter it in search of funds. This exercise is vital for two reasons. First, it forces a nonprofit to look closely at its performance in relationship to its avowed goals, and how it is perceived by its public or publics. Second, such "positioning"—as it is called in the profit sector—enables an organization to develop a strategy for attracting funds in the marketplace as a whole, or that segment of it in which an organization functions.

This strategy is a blueprint for a nonprofit's development program. It is created out of what an organization knows of itself and its market, and it incorporates fundamental decisions on where a nonprofit seeks funds, how much it asks for, how it makes its case, and what kind of communications and marketing materials it needs to make that case effectively. Once this strategy is adopted, the organization should stick with it consistently until it is either proven totally ineffective or it enables the organization to attain its financial goal. That may take a good deal of time. Nonprofits frequently are in such straits that they rush into a development "plan" without taking the time to do the research and thinking that is necessary for the creation of sound strategy. Consequently, when they are disappointed at the failure of that program to produce real gains in a few weeks, they begin rushing off in many different directions at once in pursuit of dollars, abandoning whatever haphazard plan they had in the first place. A good fund-raising strategy takes time to work effectively. For one thing, it takes time to identify potential donors, prepare appropriate materials, present an organization's case, and get a final decision on the request. For another, an organization which has been unhealthy financially for years simply cannot expect an overnight cure. It cannot, as some fund-raising consultants quite rightly are fond of pointing out, hit the track doing a 100 miles an hour when it has been doing 25 m.p.h. for the past thirty years.

Creativity, and the role of profit-motivated marketing and communications techniques, are worthy of a chapter to themselves and will be discussed later at length. It should be noted here, however, that more and more, nonprofits are discovering traditional methods of raising money are not working as successfully as they once did. This is probably because fund-raising methodology has not kept pace with the changing concerns of society as a whole, nor the evolution within philanthropic institutions in response to this change. It may be necessary for a nonprofit to redefine just who its potential donors are, where they can be found, and how it gets to them. Nonprofits generally have come to accept that fund-raising is nothing more than a matter of banging away at the doors of the foundations, filling out the endless forms for government grants, going hat in hand to the same few wealthy individuals year after year after year, and collecting fees from members if they have them. Occasionally they may throw in a direct mail campaign—without too much thought about demographic research, list testing, or packaging—only to wind up contributing to the myth that direct mail never works.

Perhaps the first creative thing nonprofits can do in raising money is to recognize that society is not static, and neither are they. Individuals, institutions, corporations which were not donors yesterday may be donors tomorrow. But it takes a great deal of creative thinking and very hard work to find these new donors and devise ways of reaching them with an appeal for support. Creative fund-raising demands that organizations not only know themselves, but also that they have some means of reading society's economic, attitudinal, and ethnic shifts. As noted time and again, the nonprofit segment of our society does not exist apart from society as a whole, and as our society changes, nonprofits too must change. An important part of creativity in getting money is directed toward a nonprofit learning how to use these changes to its own benefit.

In exercising its creative muscles, it is important that a nonprofit have the proper tools. The profit sector has taught us a great deal about how to measure public reaction to a given product, personality, or idea. It also provides us with the example of an entire industry—marketing—which has developed methods of swaying masses of people in their decisions on how to spend their money. There has been a great deal written and said derogatorily of advertising and marketing techniques. Critics blame the industry for making materialists of us all, coaxing and cajoling us into buying things we do not want or need. For many nonprofits, the industry is the epitome of all that is wrong with the capitalist system. But no one makes sinners of us; we must do that for ourselves. And if we buy cars, clothes, soaps, bathroom tissue, furniture, and toothpaste because we believe these things will make us sexier, cleaner, smarter, more individual, and more important, we are victims of our own weakness, not of an evil imposed on us from without. Anyone who will sit still for a middle-aged man singing "It's not enough to be clean. You gotta smell clean," at him from a television set and not give utterance to an appropriate expletive deserves whatever befalls him as a result of such lack of judgment.

There are only so many times that the wheel can be invented. It can be modified, adapted to new purposes, put to use in the service of good or evil. Those are all individual decisions of individual men. The nonprofit organization which accepts that it functions in a highly competitive marketplace will learn to use the tools of that marketplace to succeed in its own purposes. Just as the fact that atomic energy can be used to create or to destroy, marketing and communications techniques of the profit sector can be used to sell floral-patterned underwear or social good. How it is used, and to what end, is a decision of the user.

It should be noted at this point that there is a rather fundamental truth about fund raising that few people involved in the process want to admit. That is, while it is possible for a healthy organization to develop ways to raise *more* money, *it is impossible for a sick organization to raise money successfully.* A healthy organization is well-managed and effective programmatically. A sick one is poorly-managed and ineffective. The healthy organization has a basis on which to build additional financial support, while the sick nonprofit must first diagnose and then cure its diseases before it can hope to attract significant funding. In the nonprofit community, as in life, money cannot buy everything. The nonprofit with an ineffective or uninformed board, no structure, and no management cannot begin to approach the nonprofit marketplace rationally. What little money it might be able to raise, it will not know how to spend wisely, and will waste. With a great deal of effort and an enormous amount of careful planning and thought, a sick nonprofit may be able to raise enough money to get itself straightened out internally so that it can sustain the complex task of developing financial support. But unless an organization looks to its own illnesses first, it will never be able to convince those who have money to give that it is capable of solving any of the problems of society at large.

Sources of Funds

Nonprofits have only three sources of funds. They may raise money from a few individuals of great wealth, or a great number of individuals of moderate wealth. They may turn to institutional donors, including government at all levels, foundations, and other organizations or institutions which set aside a part of their income for the support of sister organizations and institutions in the nonprofit sector. Or they may seek support from their counterparts in the profit sector—business and industry. At this stage in our development as a society, there is simply nowhere else for the nonprofit to go in search of money.

We may someday reach the point where we more fully understand and appreciate the role nonprofit enterprise plays in our social structure, and establish other means of providing funds to its organizations and institutions. It is possible that the federal government will begin to take on greater responsibility in the distribution of our national resources for nonprofit-oriented aims. It is to be hoped that this might be done with greater efficiency and more positive results than have come out of past government efforts in the social welfare sphere.

It is likely that current congressional interest in the nonprofit sector will at least generate interest in its regulation in some form. Nonprofits would be wise to begin considering this likelihood, and exercise some leadership in its formative stages. Otherwise, whatever legislation that is proposed can be beneficial and effective only to the degree that our elected officials are knowledgeable of the problems and issues of the nonprofit community. And we all know how knowledgeable that is.

For the present, however, nonprofits must deal with the sources of funds available to them, limited though they may be. In a very practical sense, the fact that there are only individual, institutional, and corporate donors is not as much a limitation of potential funding as it is the attitudes of nonprofits toward these categories. Few nonprofits have fully exploited the sources of money within each of these categories, and some institutions rely heavily or almost totally on one group of donors to the exclusion of the others. The financially successful nonprofit recognizes that it must develop lines of communication with all categories of donors, and that it can use these lines of communication to produce additional revenue. To do so, a nonprofit must first understand something of the nature of each group and the way in which each structures its priorities, both in its system of values, and in spending its money.

In many respects, the public is the most difficult donor to deal with, even though directly or indirectly the public is the greatest single contributor to nonprofit causes. As members of the public we pay for nonprofit activities through our taxes, through the purchase of certain goods or services offered by nonprofits, and through direct donations of cash, securities, real estate, art works, time, energy, and so on. Whether or not we are aware of it, we politically support a tax structure which, to a degree, makes it possible for corporations and foundations to amass large sums of money to give to institutions and organizations that we already are supporting in other ways. And in terms of the total amount of resources spent by nonprofits in cultivating and soliciting potential donors, it is the public that is the object of the most ardent wooing. As a result, the public, which also is the subject of intense seduction by the profit sector, suffers a kind of sensory overload that makes it difficult for it to pay attention for very long to what is being said to it by the nonprofit sector.

In addition, among the men and women who make up the general population—that is, all of us—while our hearts are generally in the right place, our minds are almost always somewhere else. Each of us harbors philanthropic feels, to one degree or another, and we are willing to share what we have earned with those who have less than we do, or to organizations and institutions whose hopes for society match our own. But at the same time, we all are preoccupied with our own concerns, many of which put claims on our resources that are far greater and far more immediate than any a nonprofit could devise. These concerns are as diverse as we are ourselves, and result in our public resources being scattered among many different directions and causes. Because the public is so segmented, and because we are courted so assiduously by the profit sector, there is no unified market among individuals to whom the nonprofit can turn for support.

Thus, there is no single approach to "the public" that will succeed in attracting substantial sums of money. Nonprofits must take the time to identify and devise ways to reach segments of the population which may have a special interest in their programs, or which have a record of giving to like causes. While there is some value to a general appeal in instances where a nonprofit is involved in a cause which touches everyone —a cure for cancer, for example—organizations would fare better in public appeals by being more selective about their audiences. An organization advocating gun control will have little success among individuals who own guns, and therefore it is pointless and wasteful to direct an appeal even in part to such individuals. Our advocate group, in this case, will do much better approaching a segment of the population which does not own guns, or has demonstrated in some way an alliance with the concerns of those who seek registration of personal weapons. But first, nonprofits must be able to isolate such individuals in the general population, and second, they must be able to package their appeal in a way which speaks directly to those individuals. No matter how noble the cause, it will not succeed in attracting money unless it cuts through competing demands for an individual's attention, and speaks directly to his or her personnal concerns.

Foundations require an approach far different from that of our segmented public. Foundations exist for the expressed purpose of funding nonprofit enterprises. Although, like the public, they are segmented by interest and by the amount they have to give, foundations by and large see themselves similarly in terms of the function they serve. They are the direct funnel of profit-engendered resources into the nonprofit sector.

Most foundations in existence today were created out of great individual wealth, as men and women who made their fortunes in the profit sector saw the need to set aside some of their money for broader social good. To be perfectly frank, such generosity was given a noticeable boost by the introduction of the graduated income tax. But that fact should in no way detract from the vital work that these foundations perform. Not all foundations incorporated with personal wealth have the same amount of money to give, nor the same interests in which to invest it. There are in fact far more small family-controlled foundations with limited assets than there are massive, highly-structured, and well-staffed institutions with vast sums to give away. The 1969 amendments to the tax code, however, resulted in many smaller, family foundations liquidating their assets in a single giving frenzy and closing their doors.

Increasingly, corporations of the profit sector are forming foundations to serve their nonprofit counterparts. Many of our larger foundations were formed with the assets of major corporations combined with those of personal fortunes. Corporate foundations frequently, but not always, have close ties with the profit-oriented interests of the corporations which established them. A large manufacturer of chemicals, for example, may create a foundation which funds educational programs in chemistry, and provides scholarship aid to students in them. But many corporate foundations have wider ranging interests, including education, health and medicine, culture, and science. Corporate foundations may be totally independent in structure from their parents, or they may be closely tied to corporations, with decisions on how the foundations will spend their money being made by officers or representatives of the corporations from whom they receive their assets. It must be said that corporate activity in the nonprofit sector has shown an increase as public interest in the quality of their products and how they spend their profits has grown. While there are corporate foundations which take their role in the nonprofit community seriously and contribute generously to organizations and institutions, there are many which are little more than public relations tools to pump up a sagging public image. But then serving oneself while serving others is what capitalism is all about, isn't it?

Still other foundations are formed by public funds sought for specific causes, such as the Foundation for Special Children discussed earlier in this book. There also are organizations and institutions in the nonprofit sector which are not set up specifically as foundations, but which make grants to other organizations and institutions engaged in causes which they espouse. And there is the federal government, which often behaves like a foundation, through such mechanisms as the National Endowments for the Arts and Humanities, by making grants for nonprofit programs and institutions.

Prospecting among foundations requires a great deal of careful research and inordinate amounts of patience. The larger and richer foundations usually have broad interests, but also have very rigid requirements for the form of grant requests, and sizeable staffs to review them. They have developed rather splendid bureaucracies of their own, and it takes considerable skill and experience to make one's way through the maze of grantsmanship. But it often is well worth the effort, because larger foundations tend to make larger grants over longer periods of time. They are demanding in what they expect from an organization in terms of demonstrating need and ability, but their support of a wide variety of institutions over the years is one of the mainstays of the nonprofit community. They are a highly reliable source of funding, once initial success is achieved. This makes them worth the effort of researching their giving patterns, establishing contact with them at both the staff and board levels if possible, and tailoring grant proposals to their specific interests.

Smaller foundations usually are much less demanding and less rigorously organized. Frequently, small foundations require only a letter outlining a program or service in need of funding, a brief meeting with the foundation executive (who may also be executor of the trust from which the foundation receives its assets), and a warm handshake. Foundations of this size generally place more restrictions on their grants, however, and it is not uncommon to find their activities limited to specific regions, states, or even cities. Only rarely are such foundations of much help to nonprofits seeking funds for programs that are national in scope, although they may provide a part of the money needed to provide a program or service in a given area.

The federal government, we all agree, is a case unto itself. Since the Depression of the 1930s, the government has been moving increasingly into areas of concern shared by the nonprofit sector. There are literally thousands upon thousands of federal programs in education, welfare, health, medicine, science, culture and the arts, child care, drug abuse, and volunteer services. Each program has its own rules and its own bureaucracy to enforce them, its own complex formula for determining who will get money and who will not. These rules, bureaucracies, and formulae are subject to change at the will of Congress or the President. When it comes to creating confusion and inefficiencies, there is no finer model than our own government. Attila the Hun could not wreak more havoc among the helpless than a single grant request form from a federal agency. Like some of our larger foundations, the government is a funding source which takes years of experience to master. But unlike large foundations, there are no guarantees with the government that a funding program will exist for very long, or that the amount of money available for distribution to the nonprofit marketplace will be the same from year to year.

Just as there is no unified market among the individuals of the general public, there is no unified market among institutional donors.

Nonprofits must spend time and effort to ferret out those institutions which offer the greatest hope of support, and, as in dealings with the public, find a way to speak directly to such institutions' concerns.

There are many businesses, manufacturing firms, and other commercial enterprises which contribute to nonprofits without formally organizing foundations to carry out their giving programs. These companies and corporations may have set policies on the kinds of organizations and institutions they support, but frequently they do not. The amounts of money contributed by business and industry this way to any given cause generally is small.

Most corporations fear that if they give substantial amounts to one organization, other organizations will expect them to be equally generous in meeting their requests. In many instances, the staff member responsible for screening requests is part of a corporation's public relations staff, and does not have the authority to make a decision on funding. Corporations generally are as ignorant of the function and need of nonprofits as nonprofits are of the workings of corporations. Their contributions are likely to be nothing more than "go-away" money, donations for the sake of getting nonprofits off their backs. Often, too, their philanthropy is limited by geographic location, and by scope; corporations are prone to give to causes such as scholarships for the children of employees, or local civic organizations and institutions. Corporations usually cannot be convinced to provide substantial support for nonprofits unless they can demonstrate that nonprofit programs will in some way directly benefit them. Nonprofits which expect to garner support from this source will have to find ways to relate their goals to those of potential corporate donors, if possible. Few corporations give out of purely philanthropic motives.

One other source of funds for nonprofits should be mentioned here. And that is organizations and institutions themselves. Many membership organizations are struggling along on fees that are far below a reasonable level needed to finance their operations. Many others are giving away products or services for which they could charge a fee their public would readily pay. An organization which has developed expertise in a particular area of social concern should not feel hesitant to charge for its counsel. For example, an organization concerned with parks and recreation could successfully market its programs and expertise on setting up urban parks among city governments. Or, an institution in the delivery of health care might sell its services to communities or organizations who need advice on how to establish sound health care delivery systems. There is no rule of the nonprofit community that organizations and institutions cannot make money on the programs or services they perform. Such often enables a nonprofit to undertake programs and projects which are socially valuable, but which have no hope of being funded from traditional sources. Initial research in an area previously unexplored, programs addressed to emerging social needs, even day-to-day operations are all activities which sometimes are impossible to fund in any other way. Some nonprofits are beginning to enter into agreements with commercial organizations to permit use of their names or symbols to market products. One major conservation group has entered such agreements with a glassware manufacturer and a clothing manufacturer, allowing these profit enterprises to promote their products with its symbol and name for a substantial royalty. This is an excellent example of how the profit and nonprofit sectors may work together to the benefit of each.

Nonprofits should not dismiss their potential to raise money by, in effect, entering the profit sector. Most organizations have some product which can be sold in the profit marketplace, from publications to advice. But to raise money successfully in this way, nonprofits must be able to look at themselves through new eyes to see their marketability, and to structure themselves to make it pay off.

The Great Money Campaign

So, how do you do it? How do you go out there into a fiercely competitive market place and win? Would that there were a single definitive answer to that question. Because each nonprofit's needs are different, each requires a different approach, and different strategy, for raising funds. What proves successful for one organization, no matter how similar its structure, needs, and program, will not work for another. Nonprofits must look inwardly to themselves to find their own answers in who they are and what it is they are doing.

There are, however, some practical steps that nonprofits can follow to develop a sound funding program. First and foremost, once an organization recognizes the need for additional funds, it should make the decision immediately to go after them as aggressively and persistently as possible. Too often nonprofits take an inordinate amount of time to make up their minds that additional effort is called for and that they are prepared to make it. While boards and staffs debate the merits of seeking new sources of funds, valuable time, which could be spent developing a market strategy and a plan for implementing it, is being lost. Don't pussyfoot around with money. We all need it, we all have to have it, and it demands commitment to get it.

Second, nonprofits must recognize their shortcomings, and where it appears that those shortcomings will be a barrier to its effort, they must seek professional help. The art of raising money, and corollary crafts, has developed into a multimillion dollar industry which has attracted an array of highly skilled, honest, and perceptive professionals whose experience and insights are invaluable to most nonprofits. The experienced professional fund-raiser brings not only skills, but also a considerably broadened perspective to the troubled nonprofit's development effort. Such an individual should be able to see the nonprofit and its marketing and management problems in ways that the nonprofit itself cannot. The organization should exercise some care, however, that the consultant is not possessed of as many preconceptions about the marketplace as it is itself. A good consultant recognizes the close relationship between the profit and nonprofit sectors, and understands how to use the tools of the profit sector in the service of the nonprofit.

Third, the organization, with outside help, should determine as precisely as possible what its needs are. It must be honest with itself in totaling how much it is spending now, how much it needs to do its work more effectively, and what it will take to expand its program, staff, services, or facilities in a meaningful way. An organization also must be honest in setting its financial goal, and not shy away from a realistic level of need simply because "it seems too high," or "no one will want to give us that much money." A nonprofit which needs $10 million over the next five years is foolish to seek only $7.5 because "that's the most we can raise." This uneasiness in approaching financial problems realistically is fairly widespread throughout the nonprofit community. It generally stems from uncertainty about the worthiness of one's cause, or a lack of knowledge of potential sources for the money, or both. A certain amount of uneasiness is understandable, and a very human reaction. For fundraising is a kind of ultimate test for a nonprofit. What happens if it goes to one or more publics with a request for support of its cause, and they all say "No?" If an organization has laid the groundwork for its campaign well, if it is well managed and effective in its work, it will find financial support. Expressing misgivings by cheating on real needs gains nothing for an organization or institution. And aside from its own need to know its financial requirements, a nonprofit owes to its major donors to let them know exactly what they are getting into by making a contribution. If possible, a donor wants to know that if he gives an organization $100,000 now, that organization will not be back next year, asking for another $100,000 because it misrepresented its need in the first place.

Fourth, a nonprofit may find it useful to organize its needs into a funding package. This package is, in effect, a shopping list for donors, which outlines what the organization is doing and what it costs, and what it needs for the future. Packaging enables an organization to give a major individual donor a choice in supporting a program or aspect of operation of particular interest to him. It also helps the organization to identify the kinds of funding it needs. Some programs may require or offer the opportunity for endowment—that is, a sum of money invested by the nonprofit which returns an income used to finance its operations. Others may need funding in the form of a one-time or continuing grant. The process is useful in determining what it is an organization has to offer, and whom it can be offered to with the potential of attracting support.

Fifth, as noted earlier in this chapter, an organization must do its homework on the nonprofit marketplace, and potential supporters in it. A nonprofit must identify those segments of individual, institutional, and corporate donors which offer the greatest promise of producing dollars. It must understand how it is perceived by each of these segments so that it can determine the best avenue of approach to a donor, within the framework of that donor's established giving patterns.

Sixth, using the information it has developed to this point on itself, its needs, and its market, the nonprofit should formulate a strategy for raising money. This strategy determines which donors will be approached, how they will be approached, what materials are needed to reach them, how and what kind of records will be kept on donors and their response, the fund-raising tasks of each element of the organization's structure (and what each needs to perform its job effectively), and incremental and final financial goals. In other words, all the elements of the nonprofit's financial development are pulled together in a single plan which includes the step-by-step procedure for its own implementation.

Seventh, nonprofits must involve everyone, paid and volunteer personnel alike, in its effort to raise money. Goals should be explained, tasks detailed and personnel organized to do them. Because of their leadership role, board members have the most highly visible, and perhaps the most important role to play. They must set an example for other donors by their own contributions, and, because of their ties with individuals, institutions, and corporations, they must be the front line of the nonprofit's solicitation effort. The executive director certainly has a major role as overall manager of the development campaign, and in accompanying board members in cultivating and soliciting major donors. The staff and managers already will have made a major contribution to the effort in the way they have done the ground work for it. But they also may be useful in uncovering or approaching previously unidentified sources of funds.

Eighth, go do it. And don't forget to say "Thank you." It sounds perhaps silly, but acknowledging support is extremely important, and a simple act nonprofits frequently overlook. Acknowledging a donor's contribution may make the difference of whether or not an organization receives support from that donor in the future.

The highly complex and involved process of raising money should be treated in much greater depth than we have the opportunity to do here. This discussion, however, should provide nonprofit managers with some guidelines for how to approach a major development effort, and some of the problems and issues to be aware of in seeking support. Money is the root of all evil, perhaps, but it also is one-half of the most important management function nonprofits have.

6 ARS GRATIA PECUNIAM... CREATIVITY IN THE NONPROFIT MARKETPLACE

If it were possible to divine the formula for sound management in the nonprofit community, its one constant surely would be creativity. Creativity is the coefficient by which program and management are multiplied to produce effective results. Nonprofits each day face enormous pressures to be creative in finding solutions to social needs, and in discovering new ways to ensure their survival and growth. At the same time, organizations and institutions must compete for public attention with diverse individual concerns and the destructive materialism of the profit sector. If they are to compete successfully in this arena, they must learn to recognize the value of the tools of their profit-making counterparts, and use them to attain their own ends.

The nonprofit's most basic tool, of course, is creativity. But exactly what does it mean to be creative? We say that one person is creative and another is not, yet we seldom can say in simple terms what we mean by this judgment. We also impart creativity to certain activities and not to others, even though we are fond of telling ourselves that any person can be creative in any occupation. We also seem to believe that creativity in the pursuit of "higher" motives, such as making a work of art, is better than creativity in pursuit of material gain.

Creativity, like any other human resource, can be wasted frivolously or applied seriously to serious work. Our problem is that we attempt to define creativity, and find a place for it in our own lives, by its qualities which we perceive around us. But creativity is less qualitative than it is procedural. We speak quite correctly of the "creative process," which is the course or path that is followed in finding the answer to whatever question confronts us at any moment. There is no mystery about that process, no wonder associated with the accomplishment of "creative work." Creativity is the application of intelligence to a given problem in search of a previously undiscovered solution, or ways to utilize a known solution under new conditions.

This concept of creativity puts it where it belongs—in the realm of ordinary human activity. But many nonprofits, especially those who would rely on society's charity rather than compete for society's resources, view creative thinking with a great deal of suspicion. The antiprofit mentality tends to reject creativity, and when it does surface from time to time in the nonprofit community, it is often regarded as aberrant behavior, chicanery, or worse. There is a fairly widespread misconception among nonprofits that it is possible for an organization or institution to be too clever, too creative. Proponents of such a view look askance at the suggestion that they can benefit from the tools of marketing and communication developed and refined in the profit marketplace. Because they do not understand themselves, their purpose, or the marketplace in which they function, these organizations do not see that they must learn to intrude on the public consciousness as profit enterprises have, and develop the skills to persuade a sorely distracted society of their needs and value.

We have discussed at some length the importance of effective management principles to nonprofit organizations and institutions. Nonprofits must recognize, however, as profit organizations do, that sound management and a worthy product alone have little effect in the marketplace. The good that nonprofits do has meaning for their growth and expansion only to the degree that it is brought to public attention. An institution may have a committed and involved board, a skilled director and staff, and effective and worthwhile programs that have resulted in society's betterment. But its potential to do even more work and become even more effective lies in its ability to reach all or segments of the public, sway them, and gain their financial support. If it does not enter its marketplace with an aggressive and creative marketing effort, other, perhaps less worthy, organizations will, and it will be they who profit.

Thus, creative marketing and communications have an extremely important role to play in the life of the nonprofit. Like the fundamentals of sound management, effective marketing begins and thrives only when an organization or institution understands fully who it is and what it does. As we have seen, the properly structured and administered nonprofit is aware at all times of its internal health and effectiveness. Obviously, a nonprofit must know what it has to market before it markets it, and, similarly, it must know its potential audience—that it, to whom it will direct its effort. Based upon this knowledge the nonprofit then seeks to devise the best means of reaching that audience with a message designed to produce on-going financial support. The organization which recognizes that it is but the other side of the profit coin will not hesitate to borrow freely from the best ideas of the profit sector in developing its marketing plan, and in choosing the tools for its implementation.

There are, however, a few major differences between the perspective of profit and nonprofit enterprises in relation to their respective markets. The profit-making organization, of course, directs its attention to a market which pays money for its goods or services. Its marketing effort is concerned almost solely with current and potential users of its goods or services, and it seeks to identify them, probe their needs and wants, count the money they have to spend, discover why they prefer a competitor's goods or services, and sell its own. The nonprofit's marketing program is likely to be directed in only a small part to the actual users of its product, or programs. The nonprofit certainly has a duty to let that segment of society which it intends to serve know of its activities, and, in doing so, also informs the general public of its existence and aims. But by far the nonprofit's greatest marketing concern is those in society who share its goals and have money to give. In other words, while the profit enterprise must be concerned chiefly with the user of its product, the nonprofit, in marketing itself at any rate, is seeking to capture the attention of individuals, institutions, and corporations which are likely never to need its services directly. The profit-maker needs a consumer; the nonprofit must have both consumers and advocates.

There are, naturally enough, numerous notable exceptions to this observation. Colleges and universities routinely approach former users of their product for support. Organizations created to benefit handicapped children also must rely in part on parents and other relatives of such children for funds. Hospitals appeal to former patients, and, in recent years, more and more to the families of deceased persons who once were patients (although hospitals still are loath to admit that death—even of incurable diseases—is something that can happen within their work). But clearly colleges and universities, organizations for the handicapped, even hospitals must appeal to a far wider range of the population than those they once served or are serving, if they are to raise funds at a substantial and meaningful level.

It must be noted that the success of an organization or institution in finding advocates is directly related to its performance with consumers, and vice versa. An organization cannot survive indefinitely on the strength of its goals alone, but rather must have a record of achievement, or at least of progress toward achievement, to attract donors. At the same time, if an institution has no advocates, no donors, there is no way it can develop and maintain a product for its consumers. Thus, the nonprofit finds itself in a marketing position unlike that faced by any other element of our society. Its source of support lies not in the user of its product who more often than not is one of society's have-nots, but in members of the general population who have managed to succeed to one degree or another in our competitive environment.

The profit-motivated enterprise has no reason to be interested in the have-nots. Have-nots do not purchase automobiles or fly on airplanes or get new lawn mowers every few years. The segments of the profit marketplace are fairly well-defined and readily approachable. Nonprofits, on the other hand, are society's only organized link between the haves and have-nots. They act to better the lives of the have-nots, but to do so they must cultivate the haves. Until relatively recently in the history of nonprofits, organizations and institutions have had no other real appeal to the haves except their guilt at having somehow survived intact when others had not. But in a major shift in our attitudes in the fifties and sixties, society as a whole, rather than individuals within it, became responsible for whatever social ills exist. A single person no longer was responsible to his fellow men, nor his fellow men to him. It was society that was to blame for prejudice, hunger, poverty.

Obviously, our nonprofits could get little mileage out of guilt when no one was guilty any more. Even if individually we could not accept that we no longer were guilty, at least we allowed as how we could breathe a little easier because the jury was still out. Too, there is a great deal of comfort in accepting that amorphous mass, society, as the villain of the sixties and the seventies. Perhaps history will mark this period as the beginning of adolescence for our nonprofit community. Subtly nonprofits have begun to move from charity-as-guilt to charity-as-enlightened-self-interest in marketing their programs and services to the public. For example, one major health organization has begun to put itself through the changes of nonprofit puberty with a new slogan, "We want to cure the common cold in *your* lifetime." (Emphasis by the organization.) This is a significant step from "Fight the common cold with a check up and a check." The latter is general in its point of view, closer to nagging than to marketing. The former is addressed specifically to me and you, and puts the organization squarely in the charity-as-enlightened-self-interest category. A national girls organization also has made this shift in its appeal for volunteer adult leaders. In the past, this appeal was based on the unpleasant things that might happen to a young girl without adult leadership. Today, that organization shows us a plump middle-aged housewife talking to us about what *she* gets out of participating in the program, rather than what she is doing for the girls.

The list of examples could go on and on. Alcoholism, once a personal weakness, now is a social disease. We are all potential alcoholics, our newspapers and televisions tell us, and if we're smart, we'll support research into the prevention and cure of this disorder. In the meantime, get the drunk driver off the road before he runs you down. Mental health advocates have gone so far as to get a certified neurotic—who also happens to be a national hero—to act as their spokesman, reinforcing the appeal that any of us can fall off the deep end emotionally in our lives. Researchers into causes of birth defects, conservationists, even colleges and universities are adopting this approach to gain public attention.

These examples are important because they demonstrate attitudes of marketing and communication which have been borrowed from the profit sector. Qualitative questions aside for the moment, there is no fundamental difference between the marketing concept that says, "You need Flusho to get your clothes brighter," and the one which says, "You need mental health to make your life better." The aim of the maker of Flusho is to sell as much of the stuff as he can. The aim of the mental health advocate is social betterment. Both use the same marketing concept, however, to "sell" these widely divergent ideas.

If nonprofits are to borrow successfully from the tool chest of the profit sector, they should understand clearly what it is they are about. Nonprofits must develop a thorough understanding of the principles involved and must recognize how to apply them to their own needs and to meet their own aims. The object of such borrowing is not merely to imitate the profit sector, but rather to enable nonprofits better to communicate their needs and value to the publics they serve. Although the profit and nonprofit segments are counterparts in our society, they obviously do not serve the same function, and cannot share the same motivations, nor the same goals. Neither can they always use the same methods to achieve their goals, and nonprofits must exercise some care that in using the methods and techniques of the profit sector for their own benefit, they do not come to share the profit sector's view of our society and the individuals within it. The nonprofit segment is a balance to profit-making enterprises which see us as so many bodies to be clothed and housed, so many mouths to be fed, so many individual psyches to be catered to. Nonprofit organizations and institutions must always keep in mind that theirs is a much different role to play. While they may adapt the principles of management and marketing of the profit sector to enhance their own effectiveness, they must never lose sight of the fact that their concerns are not the same.

With that one caveat in mind, let us look more closely at the issue of marketing and communications among nonprofits. Marketing is a comprehensive word to describe the process by which enterprises gain income. In this sense, marketing is closely related to strategy, as outlined in our discussion of fund-raising. But fund-raising is only one aspect of a process that involves identifying needs and establishing programs, discovering sources which will provide financial support for those programs, devising an approach to those sources which will result in their giving money, informing the public and specific segments within it of issues and problems which should be brought to their attention, communicating internally and externally successes and unfulfilled needs, and creating and producing the educational and informational materials that will make the entire process effective. Marketing touches upon almost all aspects of a nonprofit's work; it is the glass through which the nonprofit is seen as a whole, as it interacts with society.

Communication is clearly a part of the marketing process. But because communication is the channel through which a nonprofit sets the marketing process in action, it has a special value in the nonprofit sector which it may or may not have in the profit segment. It is seldom necessary for a profit enterprise to communicate with more than one audience for any one of its products. There is no need—and no gain—for the manufacturer of computers to speak to anyone other than those he knows purchase and use computers. From time to time, the manufacturer may wish to speak to the general public—or appear to do so—to inform us all of his integrity and service. But this is done as a public relations device to enhance the manufacturer's status with his market or the value of stock in his firm. It is not done under the misapprehension that everyone should know about his computers. Nonprofit organizations, on the other hand, generally deal in products that benefit us all, either directly or indirectly. Issues of health, social welfare, education, and so on touch each of us in some way in our daily lives or in our moral concepts. While in many ways the market of the nonprofit is as segmented as that of the profit enterprise, in terms of numbers alone it is the general public the nonprofit must reach and sway with arguments for its support. Thus, the nonprofit must approach communications with a far broader perspective than does the profit-motivated corporation. Not only does the nonprofit have to communicate with specific segments of its market—or potential donors—it also must communicate with the public at large in a way unlike that of any institution in the profit sector.

The marketing and communications problems of nonprofits are made more difficult by two factors. First, nonprofits by and large deal in intangibles, as noted earlier. Even though it is possible to measure the results of specific programs, the programs themselves are addressed to intangible issues, or concepts of aims and behavior that grow out of our society as a whole. Obviously it is possible to determine whether or not a cure is found for a disease, but the idea that we must do what we can to stop people dying of that disease is an abstract social concept. Secondly, these intangible and sometimes difficult concepts must compete for attention with the immediate concerns of each of us, and the barrage of material appeals from the profit sector. As we have discussed previously, we all are bombarded hourly with thousands of competing messages from thousands of sources. Some of them are frivolous, and we dismiss them without their ever fully registering on our consciousness. Others are more appealing because they are addressed to specific concerns of moment to us, or they are communicated in such a way as to make us unavoidably aware of them. Our heads are literally full of unceasing demands for our attention and our money. Given our human and mechanical attraction to the material, nonprofits face an enormous task in not only cutting through this flood of images and ideas, but also in diverting us from our own comfort to the needs of society as a whole. It is therefore especially important that nonprofits develop their marketing and communications skills to become capable of competing on a more equal footing with other demands.

Marketing begins with an understanding of one's own organization and the many publics with which it comes in contact. Most nonprofit institutions deal with a variety of publics with varying degrees of involvement in and concern for their goals. These include:

- ▶ the consumers of their products
- ▶ their internal staff
- ▶ their board of directors
- ▶ their supporters among individuals, institutions, and corporations
- ▶ individuals, institutions, and corporations which have demonstrated some potential for becoming their supporters
- ▶ various segments of the general public which are not aware of these institutions, and may or may not have any concern for their goals and activities

The objective of a sound marketing plan is to move various segments of society from the sixth category to the fourth category, and even to the third. To do this, a nonprofit must understand how it is perceived by each market category, and determine what it is that will increase concern for an involvement in its work. This requires research, and the ability to comprehend and analyze its results. Many nonprofits are unwilling to invest the time, energy, and resources necessary to undertake comprehensive market research. They believe quite wrongly that they thoroughly understand how they are perceived by the various publics which support them, and can dismiss those who do not. But, as has been noted again and again, few nonprofits truly understand what they are doing or why, and no nonprofit can afford to dismiss any potential source of funds, no matter how remote. The very act of conducting the research alone provides the nonprofit with yet another tool for monitoring its effectiveness, and at the same time, serves as a way of bringing the nonprofit directly into the consciousness of its publics. Even if research had no such side benefits, however, there is simply no other way for an organization to know how it is seen by others and the reasons for their support or lack of it.

Out of this research and analysis an organization can begin to shape its plan for reaching its publics to increase support where it exists, and engender it where it does not. A nonprofit may find that the only thing standing between it and increased funding is public awareness. Its task then is a relatively simple one, although one that is by no means unimportant. It also may find that to increase its marketability it will have to develop new programs and strengthen, alter, or abandon old ones. It is not uncommon for an organization to discover a poor market position is due to public perception of its leadership and management. Unfortunately, most organizations are plagued by a combination of these factors which not only hinder it in attracting support, but also are obstacles to its effectiveness. But whatever such research shows, a nonprofit must believe it and act on it. It cannot ignore the difficult problems and attack only those seeming to be more susceptible to solution. Over time, those difficult problems will only return to haunt it in the form of reduced funding and inefficiency. Generally organizations and institutions in the nonprofit community will find that they must move on several fronts at the same time to improve their positions with all their publics.

Fund-raising, which we discussed at length in the previous chapter, is an element of marketing only as it applies to those categories of publics in which financial support is to be found. Among the fund-raising functions of marketing are the more precise definition of pockets of support within such categories, discovery of new sources of support among known groups of donors, and development of new ways to approach existing donors. Once new donors, or new appeals to old donors are identified, the fund-raising process is set in motion, and its strategy fully developed and implemented. While fund-raising and marketing are closely related, they are not the same thing. Marketing encompasses the overall activities of a nonprofit—of which fund-raising is but a part—and their portrayal to the public. In one sense, as noted before, everything that a nonprofit does is a part of the fund-raising process, because all its activities provide possibilities for funding. But raising money cannot be accomplished successfully unless donors have been primed for it by an effective marketing effort.

One of the most significant aspects of a marketing program is the materials and media it utilizes. What an organization says to a potential donor is a function of marketing; how he says it is a function of communications. Despite a considerable body of practical evidence to the contrary, there are no limitations on the creativity and innovation that a nonprofit brings to the creation of its materials and the selection of media it uses to transmit its message. For too long nonprofits have treated themselves and their work with a solemnity better applied to state funerals and canonizations. Fund-raising materials, for example, all tend to look alike regardless of the organization of their origin, and resemble nothing so much as the stolid, gray menu of an exclusive club that has great pretentions but only one entree. If the organization is doing good work designed to make life more pleasant, you seldom get a sense of that mission from its literature. Only a handful of nonprofit organizations and institutions seem to have realized that there are such media as radio and television, video and audio tape, and motion pictures. These media most often are rejected by nonprofits on the grounds of their expense. More realistically, however, they have not been utilized more because nonprofits' past experience simply has not prepared them to exploit such media effectively.

Nonprofits must break out of the funereal mode of communications they have locked themselves into. It is neither sinful nor an imposition to ask for money; there is no other way to get it. The audiences to whom nonprofits address their appeals do not exist apart from the mainstream of life. Those audiences are exposed daily to good design, clever copy, skillfully crafted graphics. There is no reason, except habit, why a foundation executive, for example, should have a switch in his head that gets clicked from "all other art" to "fund-raising proposals" when he sits down at his desk each day to review appeals for money. There is no logical basis for what seems to be a wide-spread presumption that nonprofit communications cannot be colorful, entertaining, and even exciting, as well as informative. Because of their difficult competitive position, nonprofits should become even more adept at exciting interest and swaying opinion than the profit sector. And no materials which reflect timidity, stolidity, and disregard for creativity are going to accomplish this goal.

Nonprofits never have been facile in the use of mass media. Only a very few organizations have begun to employ radio, television, and newspapers to reach potential donors. Even today, when television is not only a part of life, but is in fact life for many people, nonprofits hang back timorously, at best offering only imitations of commercial appeals. There are some recent offerings by nonprofits that in questions of taste and abrasiveness rank right along side some of the worst bathroom tissue and laundry detergent advertisements. In particular, one appeal for a young girls' organization has a musical theme that is enough to make any thinking man go out and bludgeon all female children under the age of ten. In buying the concepts and techniques of the profit sector, such organizations mistakenly also buy the profit-oriented philosophy that the more ridiculous and more grating a commercial, the more effective it is. But it profits an organization nothing to treat people as mentally deficient, and to throw away the opportunity to reach and sway public minds for the sake of existing standards in radio or television advertising. Nonprofits must make their own way in the mass media, emulate the best of the commercial world, and build on it to create a new form of advertising that speaks more directly of their special needs.

The direct mail appeal long has been the staple of the nonprofit community in attracting funds. Over the years, the art of direct mail has been subjected to a growing body of "rules" that determine what can and cannot be done in its use. But as the techniques of identifying and targeting audiences has been refined, and new technology for the printing and production of direct mail materials has evolved, these rules steadily have been eroded. Despite what direct mail purists may think, the only rule any longer applicable to this form of appeal is that if it works, it's good; if it doesn't work, it's not good. The standard form letter signed by a personality-brochure-reply envelope format of the direct mail appeal is giving way to highly innovative packages that employ sophisticated forms of design and construction. What in the past was found to work for one organization no longer works for all. In the 1968 presidential campaign, direct mail "experts" scoffed at the eight-page, single-spaced letter on personalized note paper devised by the workers of Senator George McGovern. It violated all the rules, and drew about $4 million. Nonprofits no longer are bound by any rules or tradition in their thinking about direct mail. In recent years, it has become fashionable to condemn direct mail as no longer effective in attracting funds. But closer examination of available data shows that its effectiveness has declined only for those organizations which have failed to use it creatively. In the profit sector, and among nonprofits which have approached it creatively in design and content, direct mail is more successful than ever.

Too many nonprofit organizations and institutions get this far in their communications programs, and no further. They utilize direct mail, proposals to foundations, individuals, and corporations, and, if they consider themselves really hip, mass media to a limited degree. But they are ignoring a substantial number of other potential channels of communication that serve well their goal of reaching and swaying their publics. Many of these channels fall under the broad general category of "public relations."

There is some confusion about the nature and function of public relations in both the profit and nonprofit sectors. "Public" relations frequently are equated with "press" relations, which are not the same thing at all. The press is but one means open to the nonprofit for reaching the public at large, or specific segments of it, and it is in no way the most important, nor the most valuable, to the nonprofit organization. The press, like nonprofits themselves, is another highly peculiar sector of our society. It is exploited with great regularity by those in positions of power, and not infrequently the press willingly, even delightedly, participates in such exploitation. Politicians, corporate executives, advocates of one cause or another, motion picture and recording "stars," and reporters themselves all use the press to further their own ends. Far too often newspapers are nothing more than advertisements with misinformation surrounding them. It is no wonder that the general public increasingly declines to share the reverence and respect for the press it feels it deserves. The electronic press is no different. It is astonishing that so many individuals and organizations fairly swoon at being granted one minute of air time just after the local auto dealership commercial and just before the nightly recitation of wire service sports scores.

The fact of the matter is that the press' chief concern is perpetuating itself as a power center in our society, and only secondarily does it give any thought to the needs of that society for information. Moreover, it is a business, a commercial enterprise created to make a profit for its owners, and it is guided by profit considerations. There is no question that the press does serve a useful function for us all, and that many newspapers are staffed by intelligent and dedicated men and women who feel a real and honest duty to report information to the people. The Watergate scandal is an obvious example of the press functioning at an optimum level in our country. But it was, in a sense, the Watergate scandal that made the press, and not vice versa. The clumsiness of a few deluded men more than anything else created the opportunity for the press to perform its self-appointed responsibilities. The point of this discussion is that non-profits should view the press as another communications tool which they may learn to use effectively in telling their stories. But it is not the be all and end all of communications.

Nonprofits should communicate with their publics directly wherever possible, rather than through some other media. One of the most effective means is the organizational newsletter. Simple and inexpensive to produce, the newsletter allows an organization to expound on the issues and problems of concern to it at length, and to exercise control over the form and content of its presentation. Newsletters, however, only rarely are timely, attractive, readable, and entertaining. Many nonprofits see the newsletter as a necessary evil which they have an obligation to produce as a service to their existing and potential supporters. In truth, the newsletter is a means of bringing information of an organization's activities directly to public attention, and a highly effective means of attracting membership and direct financial support. But to be effective, it must be produced with some care and great creativity, it must be current and attractive, and it must evolve out of an organized plan for reaching the public with a definite end in mind.

Nonprofits also may use annual or more frequent reports, letters from board chairmen or executive directors, brochures on specific issues, and other publications to get its message across. An organization is limited only by its own imagination and resources as to the means and regularity with which it communicates with its publics. But it also is important that an organization not ignore its own internal communications. Each individual within an organization is another means of communicating with the public, but each can do so only when he or she is aware of what is happening within the organization, and can communicate that information accurately. Informed and articulate staffers are in many ways the most effective communications tools nonprofits have.

The nonprofit community would be wise to begin exploring the uses of visual media to a much greater degree than it does now. There is a considerable amount of evidence that ours is becoming a visual culture, and that linear communications, such as this book, are a dying craft. Increasingly what information our society does get, it receives through visual images and spoken words. Advancing technology has provided us with the means of employing visual media in a wide range of areas such as education, health, sales, vocational training, and personal enrichment where they were used only peripherally, if at all, in the past. It now is possible at a relatively low cost to gather small groups of donors together to view a videotape or film cassette of a nonprofit's case for funding, rather than rely on their willingness to read through a printed document. In the near future, it is likely that the technology will be available for showing such material on city streets at bus and subway stops, aboard public transportation, in the waiting rooms of public health clinics, in school and public libraries, and anywhere else that numbers of people gather. These advances represent an enormous potential for nonprofit organizations, and those who wish to exploit them effectively must begin to learn to use them now.

Essentially, nonprofits must recognize two fundamental facts when approaching marketing and communications. First, the nonprofit is a competitor in a highly sophisticated, intensely pursued marketplace. Simply to survive in that marketplace requires a high degree of skill in the art of marketing, and that art is an aspect of management which no nonprofit can afford to ignore. Second, marketing can be effective only to the degree that the methods of communication employed in its service are effective. Our society is subjected to a tremendous number of conflicting images and concepts each hour of each day, pulled in diverse directions by personal motivations, and flooded with appeals for the expenditure of money for ends both frivolous and vital. Nonprofits have no choice but to develop the skills to cut through society's communications miasma and seize the attention of their publics.

The nonprofit community by the very fact of its position in our society and its past performance in marketing and communications has a truly unique opportunity to create new forms of advertising, new forms of communicative art. If it is to survive and succeed in its mission, it must be willing to spend the time and resources to do so. Because at bottom communication is much more than marketing contrasting ideologies. It is people reaching out to people to know them and, where possible, to improve their lives. And that, in the final analysis, is what our nonprofit community was created to do.

7 EFFECTIVE ORGANIZATION, A REPRISE... OR, BACK TO THE DRAWING BOARD

At this point we can begin to see that there are several attributes of effective nonprofit management which can be defined and applied as standards for measuring the performance of any given organization. These criteria evolve from the premise that nonprofits, regardless of their goals, are an integral part of the capitalist society in which they function, and are subject to the same fundamental rules as profit-oriented enterprises. In addition, nonprofits, in their present state, can become more effective only by adapting to their own ends the proven principles of management developed in the profit sector.

The criteria for determining effective management are related to five key elements of nonprofit organizations: goal-setting, structure, personnel, procedure, and programs. These elements in turn are related to and supported by two vital functions of nonprofits: marketing/communications and fund raising. The relationship of these elements and functions represents the life cycle of nonprofit organizations and institutions. Properly defined goals determine the structure, number, and qualities of personnel, procedure, and program which make possible their successful implementation. Marketing/communications and fund raising create or exploit the public attention and financial support which sustain this cycle, and make it possible for nonprofits to refine or to redefine their goals, create or expand programs, restructure themselves, and so on over and over again throughout their lifetimes. As noted, weakness or inefficiency in any one of these elements and functions weakens the entire organization, and unless corrected, will prove fatal over time.

Nevertheless, there is a hierarchy of importance among these elements and functions in terms of their impact on a nonprofit's effectiveness. There are some shocks which, like human beings, nonprofits can bear more readily and over a longer period of time than others. For example, an organization with clear goals and well-administered and effective programs can bear temporary setbacks in its marketing and fund-raising functions. An organization also may have rather unclear goals, or problems in personnel development, or weaknesses in procedure, but still retain strength and effectiveness in its remaining elements, and survive. There is one element, however, which touches on all other elements and functions with such direct impact on them that its weakness or strength can immediately affect their performance individually and collectively. That element is structure.

Structure is the skeleton upon which the meat of an organization is hung. Once goals are established, no further progress can be made or sustained by an organization unless it successfully resolves the issue of its structure. But as is the case with every other aspect of nonprofit management, proper structure cannot be understood clearly unless all other elements and functions of an organization are understood. It is not only vital that a nonprofit comprehend where it is going and how it is to get there, but it also is necessary that the organization grasp what kind of vehicle it is going in, and who is going to lead the way.

Many nonprofits, if they are structured at all, consciously or unconsciously have followed the example of the profit corporation as a model for their own organizational structure. In fact, the similarities between the profit-seeking corporation and nonprofit organizations are really quite striking, given the widespread distrust of all things profitable in the nonprofit community. The corporate model of course serves as the basis for most organized human activity. Given half a chance, a steering committee becomes a board of directors, officers, a corporation with vice presidents and assistant vice presidents. Tax laws and licensing regulations generally see the world as divided into profit and nonprofit *corporations*, in effect demanding that all organizations structure themselves along corporate lines. The corporate model has been with us a long time, and certainly has proven valuable in innumerable undertakings. But it is not the only model which nonprofits may avail themselves of, and there are many ways in which it is not an appropriate model for the effective performance of nonprofit organizations and institutions.

A typical corporate model (Figure 1) is structured along two basic lines: function and power. For example, an employee on a production line reports to a foreman, who reports to a supervisor, who reports to an assistant vice president, who reports to a vice president, who reports to

FIGURE 1. BASIC CORPORATE MODEL

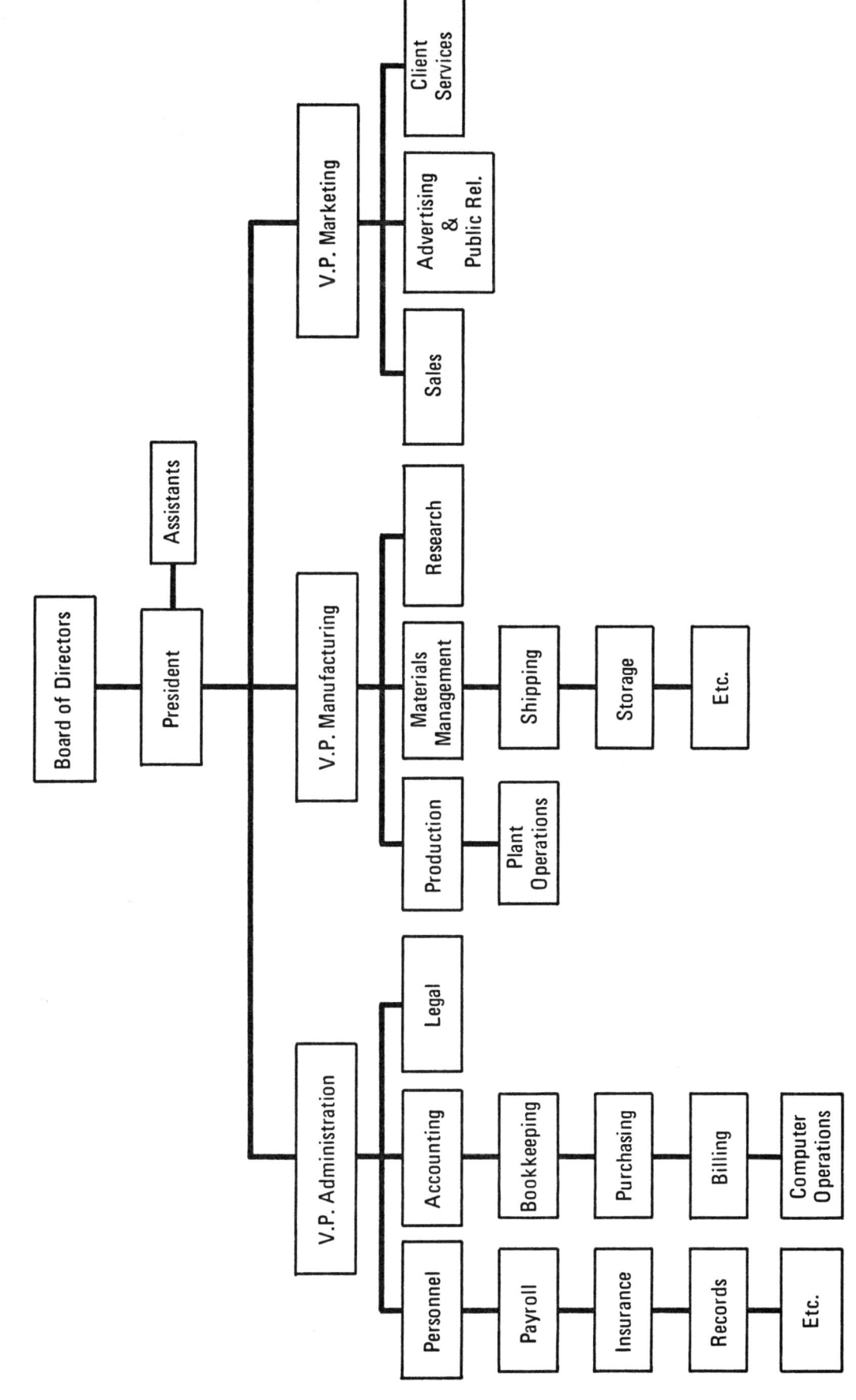

the president, who reports to the board of directors, who report to the stockholders. This is precisely a chain of command, of decision-making, or power. Stockholders tell the board that they want bigger dividends, which means that the company has to produce and sell more widgets. The board tells the president, who tells the vice president, who tells the assistant vice president, who tells the supervisor, who tells the foreman, who tells the worker, who turns the widget maker up another notch and hopes he has to work overtime just to teach those guys in the executive suite not to go getting greedy.

But there are a few significant factors in the nonprofit marketplace which the corporate model generally does not provide for. In the first place, if the widget is enough in demand, it doesn't matter whether it works, or whether it performs any useful function. There are enough people who have become convinced that they need widgets that those who are dissatisfied are soon replaced by others who will take any widget they can get. What does matter in terms of perpetuating the corporate mode is the speed with which the company can produce and sell widgets to meet the demand. The corporate model is designed to do just that, and nothing more. The nonprofit organization, on the other hand, must create a useful product for which there is a real human need. It cannot survive producing ideological and moral widgets. If the society does not need it to progress, its product will be rejected. A nonprofit consumer constitutes a minority which only in the most limited sense replaces itself as a market for its product.

In addition, the corporate model is fundamentally incomplete. In reality there are levels above and below the structure of the corporation itself which have an effect on its performance. This structure might be diagrammed (Figure 2) properly to show that beyond the corporation's own employees there exist, for example, jobbers, shippers, and wholesalers, the media in which the corporation advertises and conducts its public relations, retailers, consumers of its product, and the general public. In other words, the corporation's life, and the factors which influence it, do not end at the company gates. To take this new corporate model one step further, we find that the general public is in fact made up of individuals who own stock in the corporation, some of whom own enough of it to sit on the corporation's board. So we see that "the corporate structure" is in the final analysis a circle which begins and ends with the public.

A profit corporation can afford to relax its concern for each step of the diagram which is farther away from its chief interest—the corporation itself and its profit. The corporation is concerned with jobbers and wholesalers, the media, consumers, the general public only in so far as they affect the amount of money it makes. The nonprofit organization, however, must be as much concerned about these extensions of its structure as it is with its structure itself. For these extensions represent potential public support and money for the nonprofit, and the forum to which

FIGURE 2. REVISED CORPORATE MODEL

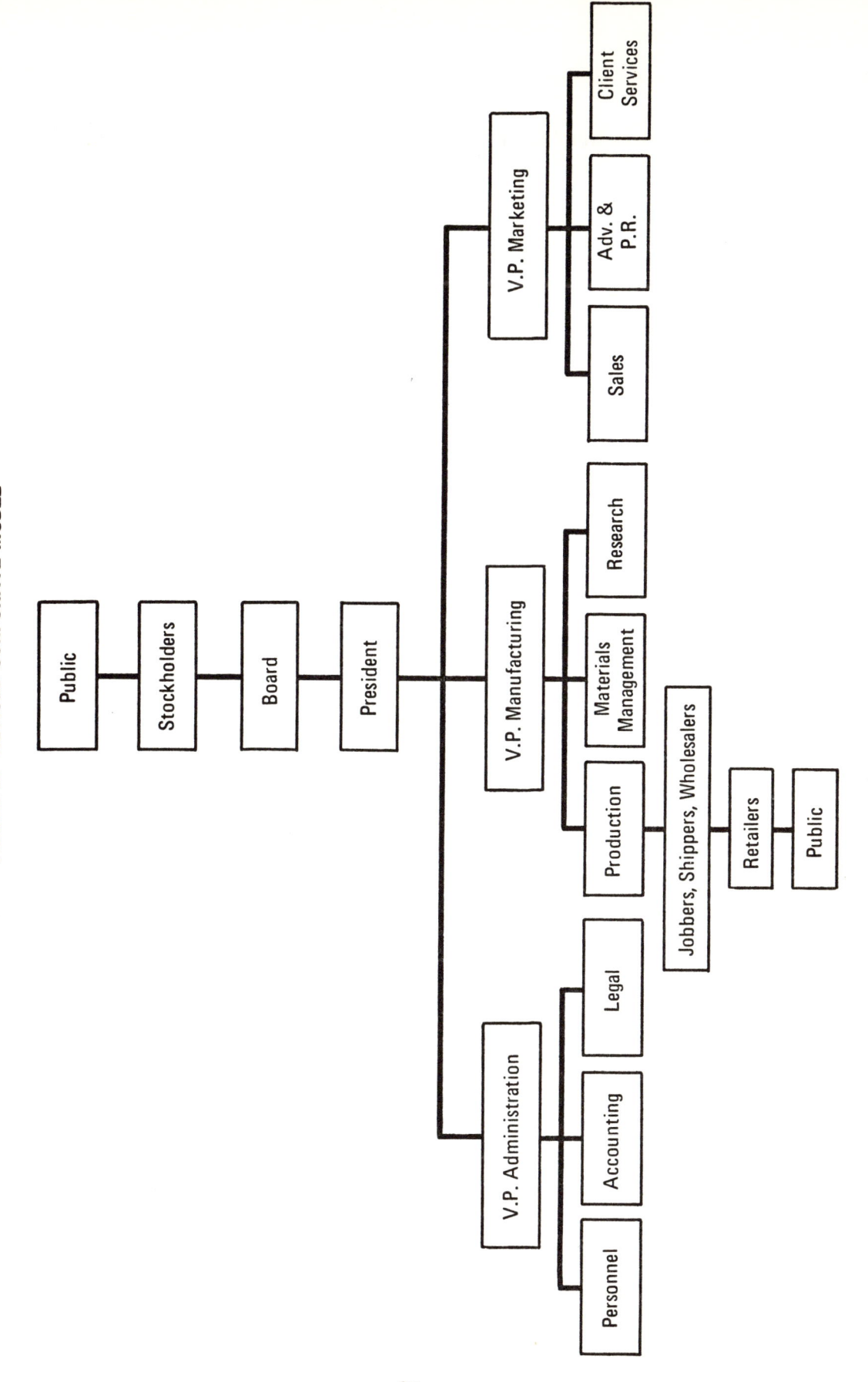

it is ultimately answerable. Theoretically, at least, there are no fixed limitations on the nonprofit's potential audience or market, except where its goals and programs limit it to serving highly specialized needs of a given segment of society. While at any moment only a relative handful of us lust after widgets, all of us are potentially a part of the audiences of organization and institutions relating to health, education, social welfare, and so on.

Many nonprofits have copied the corporate model of organization without fully understanding it, or their own needs. The Overbite Fund, for example (Figure 3), in its articles of incorporation and by-laws sounds like a profit corporation. But as can be seen from the diagram, it actually has no structure at all. It's even worse than that; through the growth of its related professional organizations, which dominate its structure and its priorities, the Fund has succeeded in interposing an organizational layer between its leadership and its programs. This layer (1) serves no useful function in furthering its avowed programs, and (2) represents a number of quasi-independent facets of the organization which only tangentially are compatible with one another in goals and function. In addition, by making its program administrators also responsible for the housekeeping affairs of the professional organization, the Fund has created a basic inner tension of divided loyalties. It is not reasonable to expect that the program administrators/executive secretaries can serve the broad interests of the public and the special interests of the professional membership at the same time. And to compound matters, the Fund's structure loses the marketing and communications and fund-raising functions somewhere in the crowd.

Had the Fund adhered more closely to the corporate model, and better understood the role of its professional membership in relation to its total organization, it would have fared much better. The professional organizations are but one element of the Fund's program, and should be treated as such. It is not really necessary that each specialty have its own organization, except to gratify the egos of those who serve as their officers and board members. By placing such stress on its professionals, the Fund makes it difficult to justify its other publicly oriented programs to potential donors and members of the public themselves. The Fund's semi-corporate model also fails to take into account in a logical and meaningful way the role of day-to-day housekeeping functions in its overall structure. The tasks of accounting, payroll, personnel, purchasing, and record-keeping all fall to one person who, in practice, is treated basically as existing somewhat apart yet is answerable to the organization.

Perhaps more importantly, the marketing/communications and fund-raising functions are relegated to a minor role. Instead of seeing its financial development as a responsibility on the same level as administration and program, the Fund sees it as another element of public relations. Clearly because of the dominance of the professional organizations, the

FIGURE 3. NATIONAL ASSOCIATION FOR THE TREATMENT AND PREVENTION OF MALOCCLUSION

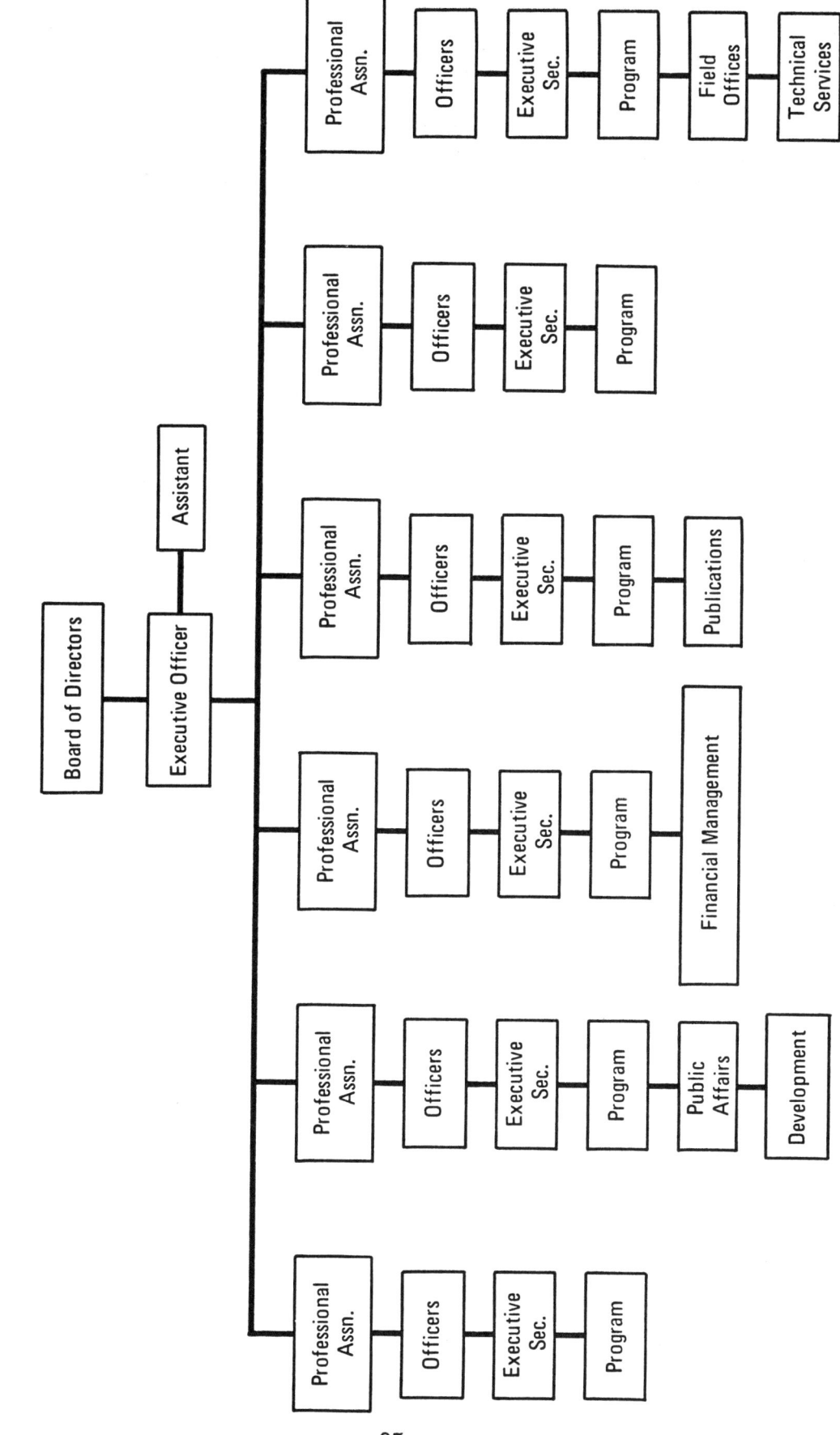

Fund has come to rely on membership fees for the major portion of its income. There is no provision in its structure for an ongoing financial development program, no provision for a manager of such a program to give it the structural weight it rightly deserves. To unclear goals, and an impossible structure which precludes all hope of sound procedure, the Fund has added weak marketing and fund-raising functions. It is no wonder that the organization is in serious trouble financially and programmatically.

The Overbite Fund can find a great deal of useful guidance in the corporate model of organization. First, it should clarify the lines of leadership from the board of directors, through the executive director and his assistants, to the managers of the Fund's administrative, programmatic, and development responsibilities. Second, other remaining tasks within the organization can then be grouped under each of these managerial posts (Figure 4). This approach serves to clarify lines of responsibility and communication within the organization, and puts both the professional organizations and financial development in the proper perspective. In addition, it also creates new possibilities for the development of a broadly based public membership and increased income. The application of the corporate model frees the Fund's administrative staff of the tyranny of serving two masters—the public and the professionals—and enables the organization to build an effective procedure for monitoring its effectiveness at several points in its structure.

Not all organizations or institutions appear to be so susceptible to reorganization along corporate lines. Colleges and universities, for example, frequently establish nonprofit corporations to conduct institutional business, and then create a very different kind of structure to manage their daily activities. The basic organization of educational institutions (Figure 5) provides for, and even encourages, a split between the academic and financial management tasks. This division, unrealistic at best, has its roots deep in our concepts of academic freedom and responsibility. Our teachers always should be free to teach, we believe, and independent from concerns over where the money is coming from and how it is being spent, to enable them to carry out their mission. Obviously, for anyone at all aware of the time teaching personnel spend in pursuing government grants and battling over appropriations with their colleagues and the administration of their institutions, this concept is pure fantasy. Not only as a practical matter are teachers deeply involved in the getting and spending of money, but as a matter of sound management principle they are the purveyors of the university's product. The only rationale a university or college has for seeking funds is the quality of its educational programs (including research). Because teachers are even more intimately involved in their programs than students, they have a highly important role to play in the finances of an educational institution.

This divided structure has two notable effects. First, it makes it ex-

FIGURE 4. THE OVERBITE FUND -- REVISED

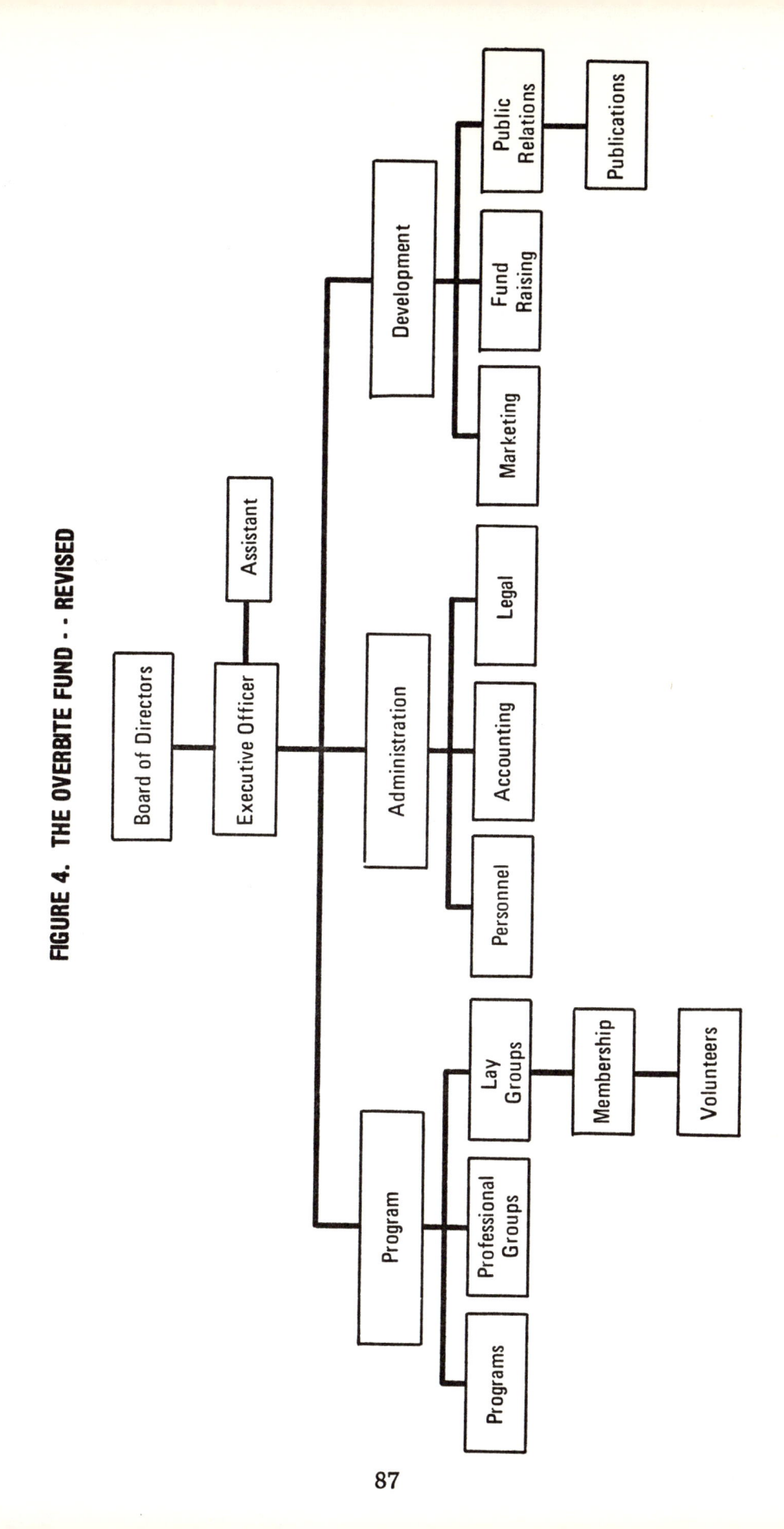

FIGURE 5. BASIC COLLEGE STRUCTURE

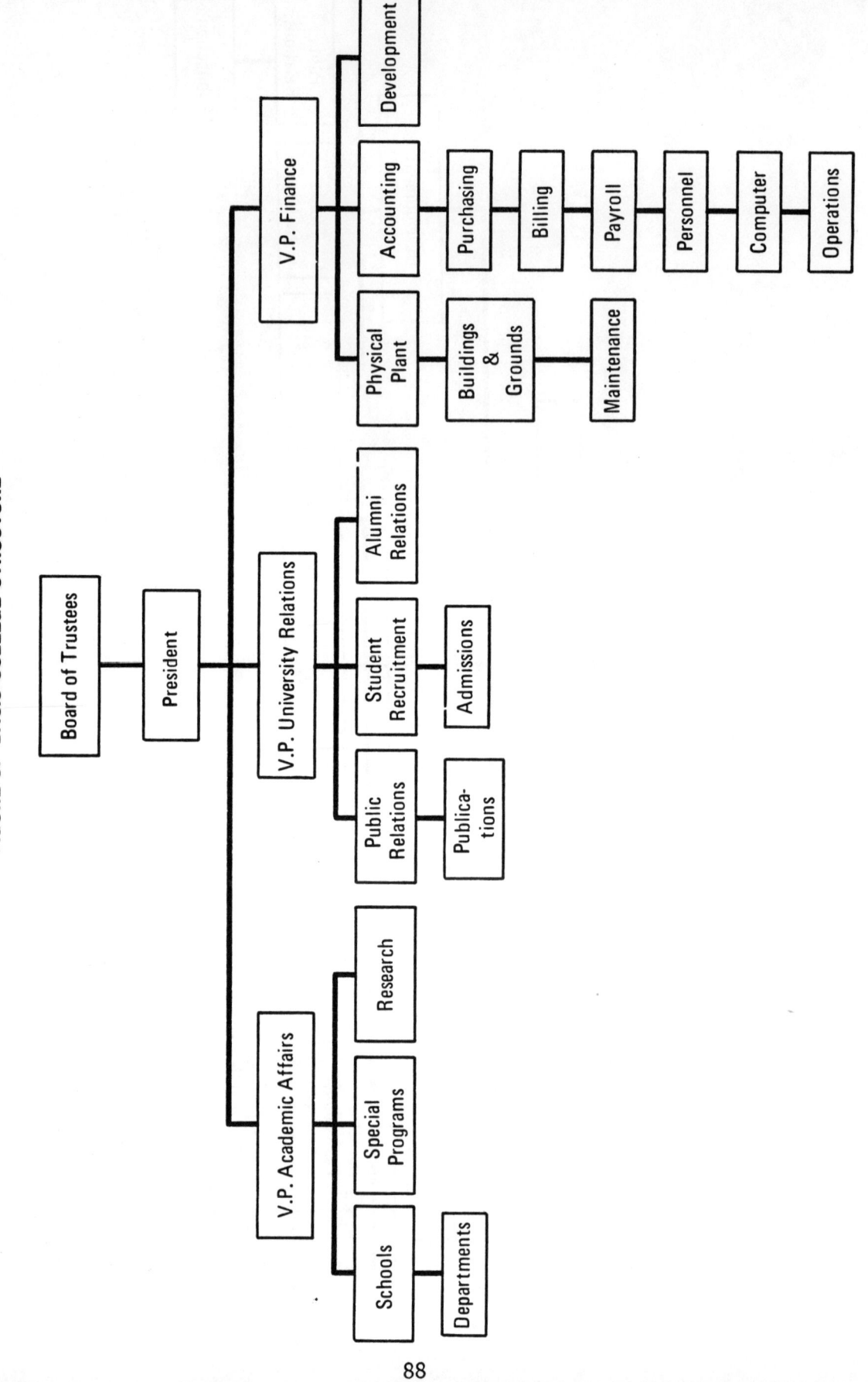

tremely difficult for the institution to maintain proper control of its expenditures and monitor their effectiveness. Since the financial managers of the institution have only peripheral control over expenditures in educational programs, they can never be sure that the money is being spent for some useful purpose, or properly distributed among competing demands for it. In addition, this structure unnecessarily creates an adversary relationship between the financial managers and the academic managers, and encourages among academics a rather sanctimonious disregard for the problems of raising money. Second, this structure places the president of the institution in the position of being an arbitrator between the financial and academic interests on his campus. The president must become almost god-like in his wisdom to decide which academic concerns will receive support and which will have to seek it elsewhere. The college president also becomes god-like in power, a dangerous situation for any organization, and especially one supposedly devoted to freedom of the intellect. He must make all the decisions because he is unable to rely on the advice of his academic and financial advisors working in concert.

Again, the academic version of the corporate model relegates marketing/communications and fund raising to positions within the sphere of financial management, rather than equal to it. This position weights them improperly with an allegiance to financial management, against academic administration. The marketing and fund-raising functions serve the total institution, and must occupy a position in which they may be carried out free of untoward influences of either component of the structure.

In terms of efficiency, it makes sense to revise this model to bring the chief functions of the institution more closely in line with one another. This may be accomplished by giving the development, financial, and academic management equal weight at a level just below the president of the institution (Figure 6). This model also groups functions of each component together under a single administrator, making it possible for the institution to perform each of these tasks more effectively and with greater control over the results. Note that all tasks related to fund raising, including government grants, private research support, and student recruitment, are treated as aspects of marketing and fund raising. Budgeting, accounting, purchasing, payroll, etc., properly are viewed as elements of financial management, and academic management is entrusted with the responsibility over programs. In other words, because it is the function of the marketing and fund-raising component to attract students and their tuition fees as well as cultivate and solicit other sources of support, the institutional structure is altered to reflect this fact. Once the institution has the student, and is spending money in his behalf to educate him and keep its house in order, responsibility shifts to financial administration. How he is educated, what programs will be offered to the student, which will be stressed and which will get little support are decisions of the

FIGURE 6. REVISED ACADEMIC MODEL

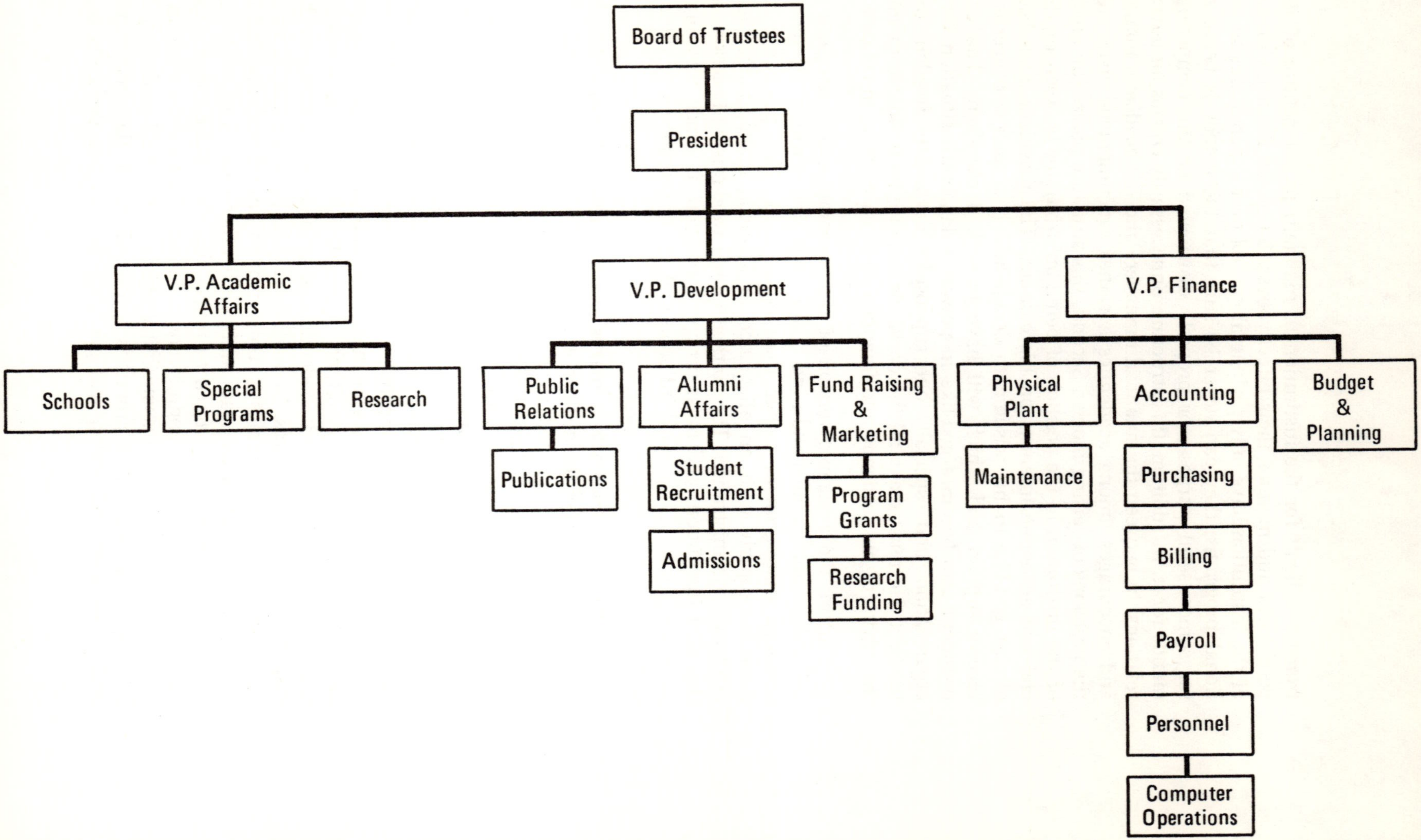

academic administrator. In this structure the three components work together to advise the president on administrative decisions.

It is not uncommon for a nonprofit organization to adopt the structure of the profit corporation, but not the principles behind it. This results in the organization developing what appears to be a fairly sound structure, but one which is in reality ill-suited to its needs. Take for example the National Association for the Doing of Good Deeds (Figure 7). As can be seen, the association's structure follows the pattern of the basic corporate model. But what is not so readily discernible is the shortcomings that are inherent in this structure when applied uncautiously to nonprofit needs and those which the association itself has built into it.

The corporate structure in this case provides for the board, president, four vice presidents, and managers of various programs and services. It should be immediately obvious that the structure has no provision for financial development built into it. The association receives funds primarily through the involvement of local chapters in annual community-wide campaigns, and ongoing media advertising by the national organization. Thus, while the association must rely on public support, it has built into its structure only the most limited means for attracting it. In addition, its management is made up of individuals who by promotion have moved farther and farther away from their individual areas of expertise. The middle management level is occupied by men and women who learned their craft at the local and regional level before moving to Washington to take their places in national headquarters. Managers who are effective on the local level are promoted to regional positions, then to national positions, then to posts as vice presidents. Throughout this vertical movement, copied from the profit sector, it is unlikely that an employee will get involved in any but his own specialty. He may be called on to help out in the event of a natural disaster, but otherwise he will have little contact with programs and services other than his own, and no opportunity to manage them. The association never has had a president who came up through the organization's ranks. For the career staffer, a vice presidency is the end of the line.

Moreover, each service is responsible for dealing with volunteers in its own area. There is no unified approach to the management of volunteer personnel, who, as noted earlier, have managed to secure a hammerlock on the organization's decision-making process. It is no wonder that morale in the association does not run very high. Because there is no comprehensive budgeting and financial management provided for in the structure, programs and their managers must compete with one another for attention and for funding within the organization. The career employee also really has nowhere to go, and when he or she does move upward, it is to assume additional responsibilities for which the employee has been ill prepared. A manager with some skill in programs for youth, for example,

FIGURE 7. NATIONAL ASSOCIATION FOR THE DOING OF GOOD DEEDS

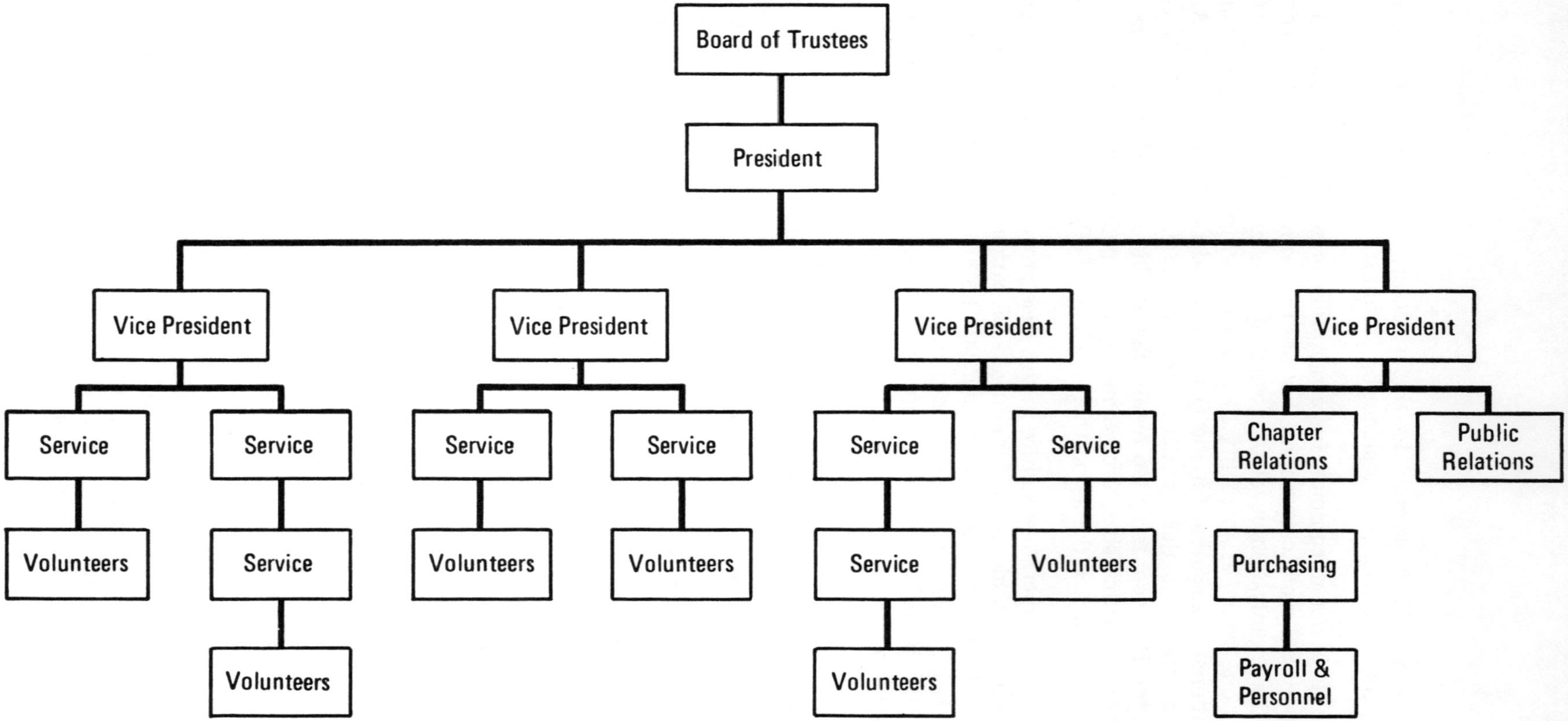

finds himself also responsible for managing health programs, of which he has only passing knowledge.

This is the inherent weakness in the corporate model, which has been discussed often over the years. As an individual rises to the top in corporate management, he becomes increasingly removed from the job to which he is best suited and in which he is most skilled. In the nonprofit which leans on the corporate model of organization, this results in individuals who are most skilled at developing and administering programs being gradually removed farther and farther from those programs. The efficiency of such an individual and his or her value to the organization begins to decline unless some special effort is made to prepare the employee for the position he or she is about to assume, or some other structure is created to ensure maximum efficiency and contribution from every employee. Other than incorporating continuous education programs for all workers, there is no way to avoid this situation in either the profit or nonprofit corporation. People will slowly rise to positions they are least well equipped to administer responsibly. And there they will remain until they resign in shame, retire, or, rarely, get fired.

Even with this weakness, however, it is possible for nonprofits to build fairly responsive and responsible structures based on the corporate model. But if they do so, they must be prepared to institute training programs for their staffs so that knowledge keeps pace with individual advance up the corporate ladder. The value of continuing educational programs for employees of nonprofits already has been discussed at some length earlier in this book. It bears repeating that such training is invaluable for the effectiveness of an organization, and an absolute necessity for an organization which takes its structure from the corporate model. By adjusting this structure so that the other key elements and related functions occupy their proper positions in relation to one another, as in the educational model, an organization can make the corporate model work for it with some success. But the corporate model remains essentially one of insularity from the public, rather than a vehicle for public involvement.

There is no reason why nonprofits should not invent their own structural models to serve their special needs. There is, after all, nothing sacred about the corporate model, and no real reason to perpetuate it in the nonprofit sector of our society. As a matter of fact, there are no hard and fast rules about the organization of any human undertaking, only guidelines which we may or may not choose to follow depending upon their applicability to our own situation. An organization's structure has only to provide for the effective administration of its programs and keeping of its house, promote both internal and external communications among its staff and administrators and with the public, and provide for future growth. Everything else is window dressing.

If we were to create a new model for nonprofit structures, based on what we know of the role of nonprofits and their key elements and functions, it might look considerably different from that of the corporate model (Figure 8). We know that a nonprofit's existence begins in the public, in our concepts of responsibility to our fellowmen and our hopes for a better life; this is the first level of our model. But not every individual in the general public will support whatever cause we are engaged in, and only specific segments of that public, including institutions and corporations, make up an organization's supporters. From the more active and more committed of these supporters an organization draws its board of directors, with all its vital responsibilities. The administration of the organization the board entrusts to an executive officer. He or she in turn sets about building an organization which will enhance the implementation of its goals and promote its prosperity and growth.

The structure of this nonprofit already has been suggested by its goals, as we know. There are two functions of an organization, however, that constitute the chief reason for its existence—getting and spending money. While the structure must be created with goals in mind, it also must take into account these important functions. These functions may be divided into two groups of tasks. The first group involves getting money, and includes marketing, public relations, fund raising, membership, and volunteer services and management. The second group involves spending money, and includes programs, the organization's housekeeping duties (accounting, purchasing, etc.), and personnel matters (payroll, health insurance, other benefits). Both these functions have equal standing in our new structural model, and administrators of both have like responsibilities, and authority.

The next level of our structure normally would include the managers and staff employees who actually carry out the tasks in each group. But because we are constructing a nonprofit organization, we are confronted with a number of issues which we must consider carefully. We recognize that because we are a small organization in which upward movement of employees is limited, we must involve them more deeply in the decision-making and administrative process. In addition, because getting and spending money are only two aspects of the same problem, it is imperative that those responsible for the management and administration of both have a mechanism for direct communication through which they may share in making major decisions. Our new model calls for a mechanism to meet both needs, called the "management group." This group is comprised of the executive officer, both administrators, and the managers of specific tasks in each administrative group. The members of the group meet as often as is necessary to discuss their activities, review programs and procedure, and reach decisions on the overall management of the organization. Of course, final decisions rest with the executive officer, but he will find those decisions easier to make with the input of the managers of his organization. The executive officer also may use the management

FIGURE 8. NEW NONPROFIT MODEL

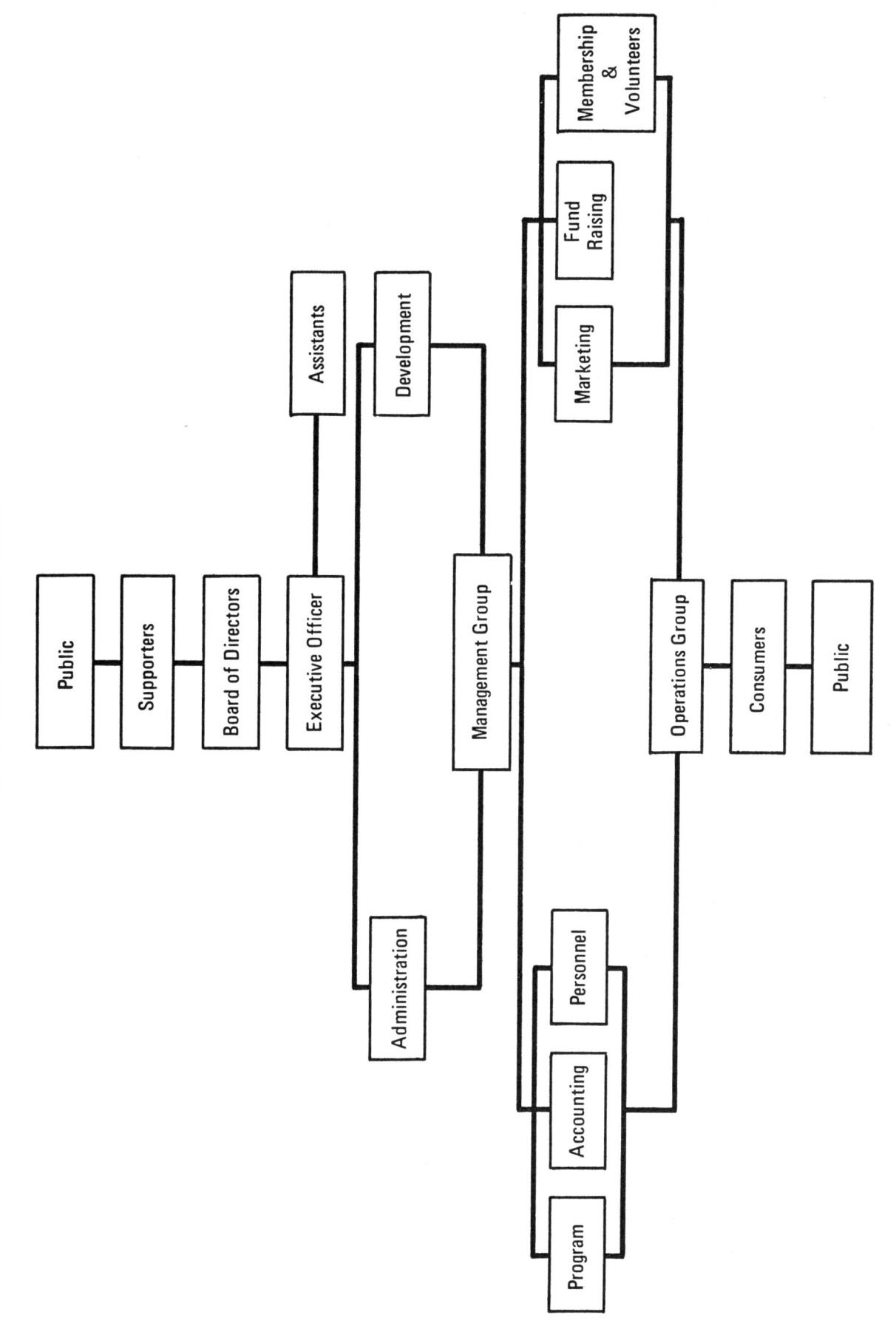

group to develop administrative talent among the managers, and executive talent among the administrators by allowing them' to make as many decisions as are within their talent and experience to make. And, clearly, the management group provides a means of monitoring the effectiveness of the nonprofit. It should be noted that the management group is more than a democratic device for giving everyone a chance to have his say in running the organization. It is a very real and very useful tool of management and a permanent and important element in the organization's structure.

The corporate model would end with the on-line tasks at the staff level. Our nonprofit model, however, does not. The importance of feedback from consumers of a nonprofit's product and the public at large has been pointed out previously. It is vital to the effective management of nonprofits that they know at any given moment how well they are functioning, and to the degree possible, the effect of their programs. This is why it is necessary to add yet another level to our structure, called the "operations group." This group is made up of staff personnel from the task components of the two administrative divisions. The operations group provides for the staff level what the management group provides at its level. It enables staff members engaged in the day-to-day performance of the organization's work to communicate regularly on problems and issues which relate to their effectiveness. In smaller organizations, staff level personnel meet to participate in the operations group. In larger organizations, where the staff is too numerous to facilitate meaningful work at one meeting, the group can be broken down into component parts and meetings staggered so that each staff member has the opportunity to share experiences and participate in decisions made at this level.

The final levels of our structure, to complete the cycle of the nonprofit's life, include consumers of the organization's product, who are, in turn, a part of the general public, who in turn, include supporters, and so on. Again, the structure of the organization reflects that its reason for existing and the results of its work both begin and end with the public.

The advantages of this structure are many. It draws distinct lines of leadership and responsibility, and, without intruding on individual responsibilities, facilitates communication and decision-making within the organization. The structure also builds in procedure for monitoring the effectiveness of the organization at two levels, staff and managerial. And, it recognizes the central importance of financial development to the health of the total organization. Perhaps the greatest single mistake nonprofits make—if it is possible to distinguish one from many—is the failure to place proper stress on development and related functions. Far too often, development is shunted off to a corner of an organization along with public relations, fund raising, publications, sweeping up, turning out the lights and other functions which are wrongly believed to lie outside a nonprofit's important work. But we have explored the fallaciousness of this point of view enough to understand that there is no work as important to a nonprofit as that of attracting resources. Finally, our new structural model makes it possible for personnel to advance within the organization by assuming additional responsibilities, and by training through exposure to all aspects of the organization's management.

Nonprofit managers should explore other possibilities, and begin to create even more innovative structural models. As our society changes the tasks of the nonprofit community change, and the new demands which nonprofits will face in the future are not likely to be well-served by the past. Goals will be redefined, expanded, and new structures will be needed as a matter of course. It appears increasingly probable that new forms of the nonprofit organization will arise from a blending of profit and nonprofit motives to meet emerging public needs. This trend already is suggested by quasi-public, nonprofit corporations in broadcasting, transportation, housing, scientific research, the legal and medical professions—in fact almost every major area except sales and manufacturing. If these new organizations are to perform effectively, they must reach out for new modes of structure, procedure, and the delivery of programs and services.

Quo vadis?

8 TOWARD A BEGINNING... THE COMING OF AGE OF NONPROFIT ORGANIZATIONS

The nonprofit community has played an important role in the history of this nation. There is no country on earth where voluntary good works have become so highly organized, and so intimate a part of the major institutions of a society. The nonprofit as a mechanism for social good is a model in which we must find considerable satisfaction, for we are creating new nonprofits as rapidly as problems emerge and new challenges are found to be met. Yet, like most things which become familiar in our lives, we have come to take nonprofit organizations for granted, and our perception of their functions has been dulled by the comforting knowledge that they are there. Unfortunately, among those who least understand why there are nonprofit organizations, and what it is that they do, are many who are directly responsible for their management.

We have come a long way socially from the time when man's only source of help in time of need was his neighbors or his church, if he had either. We have come so far, in fact, that it would be virtually impossible for any of us to carry on a conversation with our ancestors who just a few generations ago struggled to bring this land under our control. We have changed the way we dress, the way we wear our hair, how we get from one place to another, the things we employ to entertain ourselves, the kind of structures we live in, the way we seek relief from heat and cold, even the kind of food we eat.

There are some things, however, we find more difficult to change, such as our attitudes. Somewhere in our collective heads, the remnants of that prairie culture's attitudes toward charity remain alive today. In one sense it speaks well of us that despite all that has happened to our society we still retain that spark of human charity. But it speaks less well of us that, on the whole, we expect charity to be expressed in the same way today as it was 150 years ago. We know very well that it is impossible for each of us to accomplish individually the acts of philanthropy it was practical for one man to perform in the past. There is no longer one poor family in the town, or even ten. There are thousands, and hundreds of thousands, all in need of food and education and employment. Our problems have multiplied, and the number of people who suffer them increases every day. Of necessity we have channelled our charity into organizations and institutions whose public charter demands that they approach our social needs in a systematic way, and on a mass scale, with our support. But we still ask only of these organizations that they pick up the mantle of nobility that we have dropped ourselves, and ignore the central issue of whether or not they are effective. We scorn the application of profit-motivated principles we know to work to the conduct of nonprofit organizations, and encourage them to share in our distaste. Worse, these organizations themselves have become defensive and evasive in response to any suggestion that they should be effective. It is enough, they say, that they are doing the work we ourselves cannot do. To ask that they do it effectively to them borders on the outrageous.

The nonprofit community had better prepare itself to be outraged. For pressures are increasing on nonprofits not only to perform the responsibilities they have assumed more effectively, but also to take on new tasks which, rightly or wrongly, our society believes no other institution can perform. Two distinct directions in the evolution of nonprofits can be seen in our present-day society. The first brings nonprofits increasingly into the most intimate portions of individual lives through issues such as birth control and abortion. Nonprofits today are counseling, even advocating, forms of personal conduct which only a few years ago were considered not only immoral, but also illegal.

It was in fact the activities of nonprofit organizations which resulted in our judicial system viewing such conduct as now falling within the law. Nonprofit organizations are assuming the burden of individual emotional difficulties, on either a crisis or long-term basis, through counseling services and centers that are springing up in major cities throughout the nation. Nonprofits also are being thrust into the role of spokesman for all of us who previously have felt we had no voice in dealing with the federal government or the corporate structure of America. As ombudsman to the nation, our nonprofits increasingly are demanding, and succeeding in getting, major changes in the quality and conduct of both institutions. There are other areas which nonprofits are only beginning to explore and which touch directly upon individual lives. Issues such as the use of leisure time in a highly technological society, group health care, the production and distribution of food, and employment more and more are being approached through the structure of the nonprofit organization.

The second trend in utilization of the nonprofit organization is less personal in nature, but no less dramatic in its impact. As noted earlier, nonprofits are being organized and operated in areas once dominated by profit-making corporations. The examples of housing, transportation, and broadcasting already have been cited. But it may well be that we are not too far away from the operation of nonprofit organizations to produce and distribute products (which to a limited extent is being done in rehabilitating handicapped workers), and provide services, or at least lend their names and prestige to such undertakings. It would make sense for nonprofits to do so. Why not use the earnings from the manufacture and sale of certain basic commodities or services to provide programs and services for those of our society who are in need? In effect, this process would eliminate the middle man. As it is now, nonprofits must cultivate and solicit donations of funds earned in the profit sector to support their activities. Under such a plan, nonprofits themselves would generate their own income directly.

But if both these trends continue, in whatever form, nonprofits will find themselves facing new demands that they operate efficiently and effectively. If a major portion of the business of our society and the personal lives of us who make up society comes under the influence of nonprofit organizations, we are going to be very sure that our nonprofit organizations and institutions live up to our expectations of them. Nonprofits must begin now to learn the skills of effective management if they are to fulfill such new roles.

Even if the blurring of profit and nonprofit functions envisioned here never occurs, it is not likely that the demands on nonprofits will lessen. Certainly if our capitalist society grows even more capitalistic in motivation and operation, the numbers of individuals who cannot compete in such an atmosphere will increase. Over the past four decades, as our federal government has become more and more involved in the social welfare of the nation, as corporations and businesses have demonstrated rising social consciousness, the need for the labor of nonprofits has not declined, but rather has increased. It seems likely that no matter how our society evolves in the foreseeable future, life under this system will continue to take its toll in human lives, all our fantasies to the contrary. The system, like all human systems, is a flawed one, and the price we pay for its functioning as well as it does is a certain amount of injustice, a certain amount of prejudice, a certain amount of stupidity. To eliminate hardship and suffering is to change that system and make it something else. No, nonprofits are going to be with us for a long time to come.

And because they are, they had better come to understand fully the nature of the society in which they function. They must recognize their capitalistic parentage, and learn how to use their ancestry to their own advantage. Nonprofits have much to learn from the profit sector about management and efficiency, not merely because the profit sector has been so successful at what it does, but because nonprofits themselves are but another aspect of our profit-oriented society. The same fundamental aims which motivate the profit sector also motivate the nonprofit sector, but to different ends. Nonprofits do not violate their basic principles in adapting the methods of the profit sector to increase their effectiveness and to enable themselves to play the role in human progress they have accepted for themselves, at our direction. Rather, they better fulfill that purpose, and bring us that much closer to solving the less inevitable of our problems.

In the final analysis, nonprofit organizations and institutions could well go on for years as they are now, many of them barely getting by, and many more functioning at what is realistically speaking, a less than adequate level. But there is no reason why this should be so. It lies within the grasp of nonprofits to finally come of age, to grow up and begin behaving responsibly in the society of which they are a part. To do so they must find peace with the profit motive which spawned them. We need our nonprofit organizations and institutions or we would not have created them. But now it is up to us, especially those of us who labor in their service, to make them better able to respond to our needs.

Nonprofits today face an exciting and challenging future. What they can make of the future, and in the process help make of us all, is up to them. There is no greater challenge than the freedom to remake oneself. Nonprofits today enjoy such freedom, and the means to use it to the fullest is available to them. It is time they got on with it.